Natural Soap Making

"Discover The Art And Science Of Crafting Luxurious, Chemical-Free Soaps At Home"

BY JEFFREY CARTER

© Copyright 2024 - All rights reserved.

This book's contents cannot be copied, duplicated, or transmitted without the publisher's or author's express written consent.

The publisher and author disclaim all liability for any losses, claims, or financial damages resulting from the material in this book. Not in a direct or indirect way.

Legal Notice:

Copyright protects this book. This book is solely meant for individual use. No part of this work may be reproduced, distributed, sold, quoted, or paraphrased without the publisher's or author's consent.

Disclaimer Notice:

Please be aware that the information in this publication is solely meant to be used for amusement and education. We've done everything we can to provide accurate, up-to-date, trustworthy, and comprehensive information. There are no expressed or implied guarantees of any kind. The reader understands that the writer is not providing professional, financial, medical, or legal advice. This book's content was compiled from a number of sources. Please do not undertake any of the practices in this book without first consulting a licensed specialist.

By using the information in this document, the reader acknowledges and agrees that the author shall not be held responsible for any direct or indirect loss resulting from the use of such material, including but not limited to errors, omissions, or inaccuracies.

Table of Contents

Introduction 6
Chapter 1: The Origins Of Soap Making 9
Chapter 2: Soap Making Methods 14
Chapter 3: Melt And Pour Soap Recipes 26
1. Shea Butter And Cocoa Butter Soap 27
2. Cinnamon And Cocoa Butter Soap 29
3. Honey and Milk Soap 31
4. Shea Butter And Lemon Soap 32
5. Oatmeal And Goat's Milk Soap 33
6. Aloe Vera Soap 34
7. Bubble Bath Bar 35
8. Gentle Baby And Toddler Soap 36

Chapter 4: Cold Process Soap Recipes 38
9. Lime LaCroix Cold Process Soap 39
10. Kelly Green Cold Process Soap 41
11. Blue Handmade Cold Process Soap 42
12. Moonstone Cold Process Soap 43
13. Kokum Butter Cold Process Soap 45
14. Coffee Cold Process Soap 47
15. Lavender Kombucha Cold Process Soap 49
16. Zesty Green Cold Process Soap 51
17. Energizing Orange Cold Process Soap 53
18. Orange & Clove Spice Cold Process Soap 55
19. Honey & Beeswax Soap 56

20.	Woodland Pine Soap	57
21.	Sweet Pear Soap	58
22.	Lemongrass Swirl	59
23.	Mango Butter With Ylang Ylang	60
24.	Raw Honey & Dandelion Soap	61
25.	Summertime Watermelon Soap	62
26.	Vanilla Cupcakes	63

Chapter 5: Hot Process Goat Milk, Green Tea and Citrus Soaps 65

27.	Goat Milk, Green Tea, Lemon and Lavender Soap	66
28.	Goat Milk, Green Tea and Lemon Soap	68
29.	Goat Milk, Green Tea and Almond Soap	70
30.	Goat Milk, Green Tea and Grapefruit Soap	71
31.	Goat Milk, Green Tea, Honey and Orange Soap	73
32.	Goat Milk, Green Tea, Orange and Cherry Soap	75
33.	Goat Milk, Green Tea, Lemon and Peach Soap	77
34.	Goat Milk, Orange and Blueberry Soap	79
35.	Goat Milk, Lemon and Cinnamon Soap	81
36.	Goat Milk, Grapefruit, Peach and Cinnamon Soap	83
37.	Goat Milk, Orange and Olive Soap for Sensitive Skin	85

Chapter 6: Hand Milling Recipes 87

38.	Geranium Clay Soap	93
39.	Chocolate Oatmeal Soap	95
40.	Spearmint Charcoal Soap	97
41.	Orange Rose Soap	99

42.	Oats & Cedarwood Soap	101
43.	Nettle Leaf & Lavender Soap	103
44.	Patchouli Bergamot Soap	105
45.	Eucalyptus Cornmeal Soap	107
46.	Oatmeal & Lemon Soap	109
47.	Nourishing Lemon Soap	111
48.	Refreshing Rosemary Soap	114
49.	Yogurt Coffee Soap	117

Chapter 7: Liquid Soap Recipes — 119

50.	Moisturizing Antibacterial Soap	120
51.	Liquid Hand Soap with Fragrance Variations	121
52.	Foaming Shave Soap	123
53.	Vanilla Scented Liquid Soap	124
54.	Orange And Mint Scented Soap	125
55.	Natural Homemade Baby Wash and Shampoo	126

Conclusion — 127

Introduction

In the hushed symphony of our daily lives, there exists a moment—an ordinary pause amid the chaos—when we confront the unsettling realization that the soaps we use, the very agents we trust to cleanse and renew, might be laden with a chemical cacophony that whispers unease to our skin and the environment. It's a revelation that often arrives uninvited, sparked perhaps by an itch, a rash, or a quiet questioning of the synthetic concoctions lining our bathroom shelves. It's in these moments of introspection that the quest for something purer, something more intimate, begins.

Imagine, if you will, a soap that isn't just a cleanser but a ritual—a fragrant dance of nature on your skin, a sensory journey into the heart of botanical alchemy. This, dear reader, is the essence of what awaits you in the pages of "Natural Soap Making." But before we dive into the enchanting world of soap crafting, let's linger for a moment on the disquietude that brings you to this very introduction.

In the hustle of modern existence, we've become accustomed to a plethora of conveniences, yet often at the cost of an intimate connection with the products we use daily. Your skin, that silent storyteller, may have whispered tales of discomfort, irritation, or a yearning for the uncomplicated embrace of nature. It's a universal tale, a shared experience of seeking solace from the cacophony of synthetic additives that dominate the commercial soap market.

So, here you are, drawn by the siren call of simplicity, seeking not just a product but a process—an art. In recognizing your quest for authenticity, "Natural Soap Making" extends a hand, inviting you to embark on a journey that transcends the perfunctory act of cleansing. This is more than a how-to guide; it's a promise of a transformative experience—a communion with nature, an exploration of self, and a celebration of the innate human capacity to create.

The benefits of immersing yourself in the world of natural soap making are manifold, a balm to both body and soul. Picture a soap that doesn't strip your skin of its natural oils but nourishes and caresses it with the gentle touch of botanical essences. Envision a process that allows you to tailor your soap to your unique preferences, from the invigorating scent of eucalyptus to the soothing embrace of lavender. This book is your gateway to a realm where each soap you create is not just a cleansing agent but a manifestation of your creativity and a homage to the healing properties of nature.

As you navigate the chapters ahead, you will traverse the historical tapestry of soap making, unraveling the ancient secrets that lay the foundation for this timeless craft. The chemistry of saponification, once shrouded in mystique, will become a familiar ally, empowering you to craft soaps with confidence and precision. We will explore the alchemy of oils, the allure of botanicals, and the artistry of molds, guiding you through each step with a gentle hand.

The author of this journey, your guide into the realm of natural soap making, is not just a purveyor of information but a fellow seeker of simplicity and authenticity. The voice that resonates through these pages is one borne of passion and experience, a voice that understands the yearning for a connection with the products we bring into our homes. This is not the voice of an impersonal expert; it's the voice of a companion, a co-creator on this voyage of discovery.

So, dear reader, if you've ever felt the urge to reclaim a slice of simplicity in a world veiled in complexity, if the idea of crafting your own soap beckons to the artist within you, then this is the right book for you. Through the anecdotes, the knowledge, and the hands-on guidance offered within these pages, you will not only learn the art of natural soap making but also discover a profound connection—to nature, to your own creativity, and to the sheer joy of crafting something with intention.

As you turn the pages that follow, let the fragrant whispers of botanicals, the tactile pleasure of crafting, and the satisfaction of a soap made by your own hands envelop you. Welcome to the enchanting world of "Natural Soap Making."

Chapter 1: The Origins Of Soap Making

The creation of soap was likely accidental and beneficial to humanity. The prevalent story says livestock were burnt as sacrifices to gods on Mount Sapo. The fire pits were full of debris and animal fats after the rituals. When it rained, the ashes and fats washed into the mud, bringing them down to the river. As the women brought their washing to the shore, clumps of a thin, waxy powder were discovered floating in the stream. The people were washing their garments by pounding rocks on them. This made a lather as the waxy material was pounded with the clothing, and cleaner was the cloth. It was finally figured out, and the purposeful method of producing soap began.

When lye (then a powerful alkaline solution extracted from wood ashes to transform fats into soap) became commercially accessible, soap making became a routine activity. Women saved fat drippings and created soap from them later. This magnificent soap making event was an activity that took place once a year, sometimes with several housewives participating in the task. The soap was rough and gritty at times and was used to clean up everything.

The phrase "grandmother's lye soap" always strikes terror into many people who were raised early in the last century. Never be afraid; today's homemade lye soaps, manufactured in carefully managed quantities, bear no similarity to what your grandma would have used to wash out the mouth of your father when he was a child.

As with every labor-intensive job, soap making became a threat to the busy housewife's limited time and energy. The industrial revolution, which, on a large scale, transformed the Western world, has had a significant effect on the everyday life of people who cared for households and families. Huge relief was provided by washing machines, advanced cooking stoves, vacuum cleaners, and running water. Goods that were previously manufactured primarily at homes such as cotton, fiber, fabric, and clothes were produced largely and could be bought at reasonably affordable rates in stores.

Technological developments have also been extended to soap manufacturing as fairly priced cheap toilets, and house-cleaning soaps were easily accessible.

Likewise, at an appealing price-benefit ratio, all were available: inexpensive all-purpose soaps and costly bathroom cleaner, and all in between. Because the strength of lye made from wood ash has been difficult to control, soap making at home was a labor of some trials and errors.

Thus, others depended on town chandlers, or candle makers, who produced soap too. Chandlers gathered fat from housewives for cooking and butchering, produced soap, and marketed it back to home wives. The soap was expensive, however, and thrifty housekeepers tended to produce soap at home.

Like in so many other issues, soap making automation and convenience in many ways needed sacrifice. However, largely produced soap is quite long-lasting and has everything of good consistency lost, scent, form, and color. Any connection to the soap making process, along with the glycerin, is eliminated from commercial soap.

A Brief History Of Soap And Soap Making

The "new" soap as it is known to be, wasn't created until 600 AD. Soap-making factions were developed at this period too. Perhaps to refresh your mind, a faction was a community of traders or craftsmen who have ensured that their art values are maintained.

In the early 800s, soap making craft factions were especially common in Spain and eventually became the leading soap manufacturer in the Western world. This wasn't until around 400 years back, about 1200 AD, that England took charge of soap manufacturing. This was attributed to the observation of a French scientist, Nicolas Leblanc. In the late 1700s, he found that lye could be extracted from table salt before even today as a main component of soap.

Many soap makers label the onset of modern handcrafted soap making renaissance with Ann Bramson's 1972 publishing of a small book, named Soap. Ever since, soap making has developed considerably in art, design, hobby, and industry, and people around the world are experiencing the same pleasure that those legendary washerwomen of Mount

Sapo would have felt when they found the delight of handmade soaps.

What Is Soap Making?

World War 1 contributed to the usage of synthetic detergents, and the scarcity of easily available animal fat demanded a particular supply of fatty acids for homemade soap. To this purpose, we use vegetable oils today. Moreover, the ashes used throughout history were modified, and the active ingredient extracted and today we use sodium hydroxide.

For hundreds of years, people have produced soap to help clean dirt and oil from their bodies, dishes, surfaces, floor, or clothes. Individuals have needed to produce soap at home in the past, as it was not available in stores. At home, soap making was a time-consuming, messy, and hot procedure that many people performed only once a year.

What About 21st Century Soaps?

Currently, the industrial soap that you and your family are using follows a standard formula and is also being manufactured in a pretty close manner as it was about a hundred years earlier, shortly after the industrial revolution. However, the ways the producers have changed involve rendering soap milder on the skin, soap coloring, and its scent.

How Soap Products Became Popular

Entrepreneurs in many geographical regions have established factories to produce specialized soaps with a transparent type with a distinctive and delicate fragrance.

Since people also needed laundry soap, manufacturers started grinding soap with a mortar and pestle to make flakes that rapidly dissolved in warm water. By the late 18th century, soap making became a huge business with the opening of large industries in major cities. Many of those industries still operate today, producing various soaps and laundry types. Intensive advertisement for soap in newspapers and magazines caused individuals to buy soaps in retail shops quickly.

Chapter 2: Soap Making Methods

There are five methods available for making your own soap. Two of these techniques entail beginning anew and encouraging the chemical reaction that transforms other materials into a novel soap. The other two approaches entail taking pre-existing soaps and transforming them into novel creations. You might want to try out each technique when you start creating soap to see which one you like most. The five methods for creating soap are:

- Cold process
- Hot process
- Melt and pour process
- Liquid soap making
- Re-batching or Hand Milled

The Cold Process

Remember that the cold process is the highest level of all the soap-making processes. The gameplay gets a little more intricate, but don't worry—we've got you covered and will walk you through every step of the way. The benefit is that you can incorporate as many colors, shapes, and natural elements as you choose into your finished design. Furthermore, you may rest assured that your soap is created entirely at home.

Let's begin with the basic components required for cold process soapmaking.

- distilled water with lye flakes
- A source of fat, be it vegetable oil or animal fat
- Your selected natural soap dye, in either a liquid or powder form (optional but preferred)
- Soap pot and additional equipment, which we will talk about in more detail soon
- fragrance or your chosen essential oil (optional but preferred)
- a mold in the shape you want
- a spotless workspace and a cool, dry location to allow the soap to cure
- For visual appeal, use flowers or exfoliants (optional)

How It Works

Preparing lye and a source of fat and combining them is the core of the cold soap production process.

1. Making The Lye Solution

Making the lye solution is the first step. You'll need to consult your selected recipe for precise measurements.

Place the glass pitcher on your kitchen scale or digital scale, then reset the scale to zero. After that, you would add distilled water as your recipe instructed. Because some recipes call for weight, you will put the pitcher on the scale. Since some recipes specify volume, you can use your measuring cup with those.

The lye needs to be measured next. Use your mason jar, which has a tight, secure lid, to do this. Lye is an alkali that can cause skin irritation. Because of this, you must handle it with safety goggles on and gloves on. Take off any lye flakes that stick to your glove right away. Set the scale to zero and place the Mason jar and lid on it. When the scale reads the weight specified in your selected recipe, add the lye flakes. You can use a plastic pitcher in place of the Mason jar. But save this pitcher for handling lye only—use it for nothing else when manufacturing soap.

It's time to combine your weights after they have been adjusted as per the recipe. But proceed with caution. Be careful not to pour water directly into the lye, but rather to gradually add the lye to the water. Start slowly pouring the lye flakes into the water-filled pitcher. To prevent splashes, add it gradually and from a close but safe distance. Again, without splattering, stir the mixture slowly and gently to dissolve the lye as needed. It's natural to start hearing fizzing sounds or feeling heat as the two react. Keep the solution away from your skin's direct contact. Wear gloves and goggles at all times. As soon as you're done stirring, wash the tool you used. Remember to cover and allow to settle for a while the pitcher with your freshly combined lye water. Ensure that it is safely stored away from children and pets and that it is tied securely. Lye and lye water should always be handled carefully..

2. Preparing Oils

Get out your handy scale once more because we'll weigh out the oil of your choice in accordance with the formula. We'll use the same technique of placing a glass pitcher or soap pot on the scale and setting it to zero. For solid oils like cocoa butter, it is best to use the soap pot; for liquid oils like olive oil, use the glass pitcher. Add oil to your container little by little until the scale registers the required weight.

Sources of solid fat examples are: Cocoa butter, palm, or coconut

Sources of liquid fat include castor, canola, olive, and sunflower oils.

Use a sauce pan to first melt any solid oil you may be using. This will save you time because you already need to heat the oil of your choice. Turn up the heat to medium and swirl slowly because the oil needs to heat up gradually. Using the thermometer, you must monitor the oil's temperature and cut off the heat when it approaches 110 degrees Fahrenheit. It cannot, however, be added to the lye water combination just yet. The oil must cool to 100 degrees Fahrenheit in order to combine with the lye water. Make sure all of the solid oil has melted if you're using it. If the recipe calls for a combination of liquid and solid fats, add the liquid oils after the solid fats have melted completely. But keep an eye on your temperature once again because doing so will cause the oil mixture's temperature to drop. Recall that it must be approximately 100 degrees Fahrenheit when combined with the lye water..

3. Add Lye Water To The Oil Base

When you combine these two, a chemical reaction between the lye and oil reacts in the presence of heat to produce soap. This reaction is known as saponification, and it will happen instantly. The mixture will also become hazy. Since the lye was converted to soap when it was combined with the heated oil, it is no longer chemically lye and is therefore safe for skin contact in homemade soap. You need to have your preferred additions ready, such as your fragrance bottles, essential oils, dye, spatulas, etc., as the process will move swiftly from this point on.

Carefully pour the lye mixture into the soap pot's heated oil. The mixture will begin to cloud, and you will notice a change in color. Gently stir, ideally using a stick blender; but, at this stage, keep it off. Once all of the lye water combination has been added, store the glass pitcher in a secure location until you have had time to clean it properly. You must stick with your new blend for the time being.

If you are using a stick blender, turn it on right now and let it blend the mixture for brief intervals of a few seconds. Continue doing this until you are satisfied that the oil and lye have combined thoroughly and you have reached trace. Trace is reached after the combination has emulsified, therefore if the mixture is left later, the process will continue to cause it to get thicker and thicker over time..

How To Know If You Have Reached Trace Point?

The saponification process has been significantly accelerated by the stick blender; instead of taking hours with frequent swirling, achieving trace now only takes seconds. The oil and lye water have not yet fully combined if your mixture still has shimmering, oily liquid floating between strokes. When the creamy consistency begins to somewhat thicken and becomes uniform rather than having both thick and greasy consistencies, you will have reached trace..

Why Is It Important To Reach Trace Point?

For a number of reasons, the main one being that dumping the mixture before reaching the trace leads in incomplete soap, as the tracing point is the point at which all of the mixture has emulsified and turned into soap particles rather than oil and lye. This will result in partially or badly made soap. Furthermore, the soap still contains lye particles, which are extremely damaging to your skin. As a result, you must whisk continuously until the batter has the consistency of thin cake and there are no visible oil streaks. There won't be any oil spilling from the batter, and this mixture will be uniformly thick and easy to pour into a mold.

Before starting the thick medium trace stage, it is okay to apply your aroma and color during the light trace step. Compared to light trace, medium trace has a thicker consistency more akin to pudding. If you pour a small amount of the batter from the blender into the combination, you can see visible soap streaks on the mixture's surface, similar to how chocolate streaks on cake. Now is the best time to incorporate your hard natural additions, including petals, leaves, and exfoliants.

The final trace consistency has a thick pudding batter-like appearance. You want that trace consistency, which is what will make the material take on its shape when it is poured into a mold. You must continue to swirl with the stick blender in order to reach this trace stage. To acquire the soap consistency needed for frosting or ornamental uses, you will need to thicken your trace significantly if you want to make soap icing.

Remember this crucial false trace indication. When using a solid trace, if it hasn't been completely melted and heated, it can readily cool down during mixing, giving the impression that the mixture is hardening when, in reality, the solid fat is hardening rather than saponification. Therefore, be sure to cook it sufficiently..

Factors That Can Affect Trace Consistency

Without a doubt, compared to hand stirring, using a stick will enable you to attain a medium and thick consistency much more quickly. When you achieve thin trace consistency, you can use a spatula to stir by hand to give your dye and aroma time to blend.

Certain additions and scents, like clay, quicken the trace process and cause your mixture to thicken quickly. Think carefully about these ingredients, as well as when and how to stir. After adding a fragrance, it is best to turn the stirring back to manual.

The Hot Process

This method is similar to the cold method, except instead of doing the soap "cooking," it is done with heat pots. The hot process recipes in the second section of this book have more thorough instructions..

The Melt and Pour Method

This method saves a significant amount of time and is among the simplest for manufacturing soap. In this method, you can skip the time-consuming step of mixing fats with an alkali like lye and instead utilize a manufactured soap base that has already gone through the saponification process. Fatty acids and glycerin are found in a ready-made soap foundation, along with other natural components.

If you're new to the arena, still getting to know it, and want to be cautious, the melt and pour method is ideal. Instead of creating the soap from scratch, all you need to do is buy pre-made solid soap base, and once it hardens, you can use it right away. There is no need to wait for an unnecessary amount of time to pass, as there is with cold process soap.

How this approach functions

Look for a prepared soap foundation at your local arts and crafts store. The clear glycerin or white prepared soap bases are among the greatest possibilities available for purchase. A bar of soap is not the same and can cause you problems when melting, so avoid using it for this purpose.

Melting your solid manufactured soap base would be the next step. Slice the bar into tiny 1-inch pieces with a sharpened knife to expedite this process. Here, accuracy in measurements is not important. Smaller bits will melt more quickly than one giant lump, thus that's the desired outcome.

Place your chopped portions in a microwave-safe dish and zap for 30 seconds. Remove the dish, stir the melted contents, reheat it for a further 30 seconds, and then remove it once more to stir. Until the consistency of your melted soap base is entirely liquid with no lumps or hard chunks in between, repeat this cycle of 30 seconds heat and stirring. At that point, the soap base has completely melted. Don't heat it up any more than that.

If you don't have a microwave in your home, you may still make a water bath by using a saucepan filled with water instead of the microwave. After heating the water, place a glass bowl in it and let it to float. Place the chunks of soap base into the glass bowl and allow the heat from the hot water to seep into the bowl, causing the chunks of soap base to melt beautifully. Remember to stir. When the soap base is totally melted and lump-free, remove the bowl from the sauce pan.

Allow your soap to melt and the temperature to drop to about 50 degrees. When the melt is still hot, avoid adding your dye or essential oils. Don't allow it to cool down to the point of solidification either. Depending on the desired color strength, add two to three drops of your chosen dye. If you're using a powdered dye, dissolve two to three tablespoons of the powder in a little amount of liquid glycerin before adding it to the melt to prevent uneven color distribution. A nice aroma is always a great addition to your soap. You can add about 15 g of fragrance oil or half a tablespoon of essential oil for every pound of soap. To guarantee they are gentle and kind to your skin, use the ones marked "soap making" rather than "candle oils."

Before the final step, mix in all of the added color and aroma drops. The next step is to pour your scented and colored melt into the mold of your choosing and allow it to cool naturally for a period of 12 to 24 hours. Once the soap has fully set, remove it from the mold and it's ready to use right away. However, confirm that the borders are fully dry..

The Liquid Soap Making Process

We will need to utilize potassium hydroxide rather than sodium hydroxide to manufacture homemade liquid soap. Hard soap is made of sodium hydroxide, while liquid soap is made of potassium hydroxide. Instead of coming in beads, potassium hydroxide is sold in flakes, which dissolve much more readily than beads. Learning how to manufacture liquid soap comes next, after one has mastered the art of making solid soap. You can use liquid soap as dish soap, body wash, and shampoo. Additionally, it can be used to wash clothing..

Equipment for making liquid soap:

- Blender Crockpot Stick
- Potato masher; plastic stirrer or spatula; digital kitchen scale
- Goggles and gloves
- Plastic receptacles
- Thermometer

The Rebatching (Hand-Milling) Method

Hand-milling, sometimes referred to as rebatching, is another quick and simple process. As the name implies, it's frequently used to rebatch, or use the soap you made, in case there were any errors or in case you messed up the mold during the design phase or didn't like its shape. If you want to try creating soap at home without having to acquire extra equipment, you may also utilize this method. You can utilize pre-existing soap for that purpose. But since premade soap never melts easily, even though you heat it as we mentioned in the melt and pour method, you will first soften the mixture with a few table spoons of water, glycerin, etc. Wearing heat-resistant gloves, you will then add your melted soap to a Ziploc bag and knead it until it becomes mushy.

You can add the fragrance and color to your mixture using the rebatching method, just like in the melt and pour method, and then allow it to harden. But while you wait for all the water to evaporate, this will take five to seven days. Don't use the freezer out of impatience. Rebatched soap is a good way to fix destroyed soap or to add your own color and scent to already-existing soap, even though it doesn't have the most beautiful appearance or texture. Additionally, this method avoids the disadvantage of adding materials that are damaged by lye, including lavender buds that turn brown when exposed to lye. Additionally, colors that are incompatible with the cold process due to their sensitivity to lye's pH can be used. Similar to this, mild fragrances that are disguised when employed in the cold process can be used with the rebatching approach.

Both the rebatching and the melt and pour procedures have the advantage of not requiring you to deal with lye, which is a powerful alkali and is hated by many. Furthermore, you may start enjoying the soap right away after it solidifies without needing to complete complicated calculations or use a lot of components. On the other hand, because you are starting with something that someone else manufactured and not creating everything from scratch as with the cold approach, you have very little control over the raw ingredients used. The cold process is the perfect method for you if you want to be the experiment's master and have complete control over what ingredients go into your soap.

Chapter 3: Melt And Pour Soap Recipes

1. Shea Butter And Cocoa Butter Soap

Equipment:

- Bowls
- 1 mold (large)
- Silicon spatula
- Knife
- Hand blender
- Small spoon (for decoration)

Ingredients:

- Lard – 250 g
- Coconut oil – 140 g
- Shea butter – 200 g
- Olive oil – 100 g
- Lye – 150 g
- Water – 200 g
- Essential oil (of your choice) 5 g

Directions:

1. Put the butters and the lard into a bowl and melt them in the microwave for about 30 seconds. Melt them for longer if needed to make sure that they are the right consistency.
2. Mix them together with a spoon to combine them evenly.
3. Add all of the oils into another bowl and stir them evenly.
4. Add the essential oil of your choice to the oil bowl and stir again.
5. Mix everything together in a big bowl.
6. Use a hand blender to achieve the right consistency for soap.
7. Pour the mixture into one large mold.
8. Leave the soap inside the mold for 24 hours.
9. When the soap has properly hardened, remove it from the mold.
10. Use the small spoon to create decorations across the soap. You can do this by dragging the spoon over the soap to create zig zag marks.
11. With a knife, cut the soap into thick slices.
12. Return the soap in a dark and dry place and leave it for two weeks to harden and for the water to evaporate.

2. Cinnamon And Cocoa Butter Soap

Equipment:

- Bowls
- Knife
- Silicon spatula
- Long rectangular mold
- Hand blender

Ingredients:

- Castor oil – 200 g
- Cocoa butter – 150 g
- Coconut oil – 160 g
- Olive oil – 120 g
- Lye – 200 g
- Water – 130 g
- Cinnamon essence oil – 5 g

Directions:

1. Place the fragrance oil into a separate small bowl.
2. Carefully mix the lye and the water together. Gently stir with the spatula until they are mixed well together.
3. Melt the coca butter in the microwave for about 30 seconds, or however long it takes to get it to the right consistency.
4. Add the butter and all the other oils into a new bowl and mix them all together with the spatula.
5. Combine everything together into a large bowl.

6. Use a hand mixer to blend everything together until you achieve the right consistency.
7. Pour the mixture into the mold.
8. Let the soap sit in the mold for three days.
9. Remove the soap from the mold and cut it up into your desired slices.
10. Place the soap into a dark and dry place and wait for about four weeks before using the soap.

3. Honey and Milk Soap

Equipment:

- Bowls
- Silicon spatula
- Honeycomb mold
- Hand blender

Ingredients:

- Milk base soap base – 500 g
- Honey – 75 g

Directions:

1. Melt the soap base in the microwave for about 30 seconds or however long it takes to melt it to a liquid texture.
2. Add the honey to the mixture and stir until everything is properly combined.
3. Pour the mixture into the honeycomb molds.
4. Let the soap cool for about two hours.
5. Remove the soaps from their molds and leave them to dry for another 48 hours before using them.

4. Shea Butter And Lemon Soap

Equipment:

- Bowls
- Silicon spatula
- Individual soap molds
- Hand blender

Ingredients:

- Shea butter soap base – 500 g
- Food color of your choice – 5 g
- Lemon essential oil –10 g

Directions:

1. Add the pre-made soap base to a microwave bowl.
2. Melt it in the microwave in 30 second increments until the mixture is completely smooth.
3. Leave the mixture to cool a little.
4. Add the food color of your choice and make sure that everything is mixed together properly.
5. Next add the essential oil and stir it all together until smooth.
6. Pour the mixture into the molds.
7. Leave the soap in the mold for 24 hours.
8. Remove the soaps from the molds and leave them in a dark and dry place.
9. Wait for about three weeks before you use them.

5. Oatmeal And Goat's Milk Soap

Equipment:

- Bowls
- Silicon spatula
- Individual soap molds
- Hand blender

Ingredients:

- Honey 10 g
- Goat's milk soap base – 500 g
- Oats – 100 g
- Almond essential oil – 5 g
- Vitamin E capsule – 2 capsules

Directions:

1. Start by placing the pre-made goat's milk base soap into a bowl that you can use in the microwave.
2. Melt it in the microwave until it is completely liquid. Then let it cool a little to the side.
3. Add the raw oats into the mixture.
4. Using a spatula, gently mix in the oats into the mixture. Make sure that you have everything combined together properly.
5. Add the almond essential oil and the Vitamin E capsules.
6. Using the spatula, mix everything together until the Vitamin E capsules dissolve completely.
7. Pour the soap into the molds.
8. Let the molds sit for 48 hours.

6. Aloe Vera Soap

Equipment:

- Bowls
- Silicon spatula
- Individual soap molds
- Hand blender

Ingredients:

- Water – 200 g
- Aloe Vera – 50 g
- Lye – 300 g
- Olive oil – 150 g
- Coconut oil – 90 g

Directions:

1. Combine the water and the lye into a bowl. As always, make sure that you do this very carefully and that you take care of your eyes, your lungs and your skin.

2. Mix the oils together in another bowl until everything is properly combined together.
3. Pour the oils into the lye and water mixture.
4. Using the hand blender, combine the two mixtures together until you get the consistency that you like.
5. Pour the mixture into individual soap molds and leave them for 48 hours.
6. Remove the soaps from the molds.
7. Leave them in a dark and dry place for three weeks before using.

7. Bubble Bath Bar

Equipment:

- Bowls
- Silicon spatula
- Individual soap molds
- Hand blender

Ingredients:

- Baking soda – 200 grams
- Essential oil of your choice – 5 g
- Coconut oil – 100 g
- Liquid soap or bubble bath – 100 g
- Corn starch – 100 g
- Food color – a few drops

Directions:

1. Mix all the dry ingredients together until everything is evenly combined.
2. Add all of the liquid ingredients into it but leave out the essential oil and the food color.
3. Stir everything until you get a creamy, even mixture.
4. Pour the mixture into the individual soap molds of your choice.
5. Leave the soap to harden for about 48 hours.
6. Remove the soup from the molds.
7. Put the molds in a dark and dry place and leave them for about two weeks before using.

8. Gentle Baby And Toddler Soap

Ingredients and equipment:

- 5.29 ounces Goat's milk melt and pour soap
- 2.5 g organic calendula extract
- 2.5 g hydrolyzed oats
- 20 drops tangerine essential oil

For preparing and storing:

- A pair of disposable gloves
- Apron
- Weighing scale
- Wax paper
- 2 small, silicone soap molds
- Funnel pitcher (microwave safe)
- Knife
- Spatula
- Cling wrap
- Cutting board

Directions:

1. Wear the apron and gloves. Place all the equipment and ingredients close to you on your countertop.
2. Weigh the ingredients one at a time. Make sure that the weighing scale shows zero before measuring each ingredient.

3. Place the cutting board on your countertop. Place the wax paper over the cutting board. Place the soap base on the wax paper and chop into ½ inch pieces.
4. Lift the wax paper along with the soap pieces and pour into the funnel pitcher. Place the pitcher in the microwave and cook on high for 1 – 2 minutes or until it melts. Stir every 30 seconds until it almost melts after which, stir every 10 seconds until it just melts.
5. Stir in the essential oil and stir. Cook in the microwave for 10 to 20 seconds if required, stirring after 10 seconds.
6. Transfer the soap mixture into the soap molds or use one larger mold. This is done to remove extra bubbles. Set the molds aside for 12 – 24 hours.
7. Remove the soap from the molds (wearing gloves). In case the soap is not coming out of the molds easily, freeze for 60 – 70 minutes. It will come out easily.
8. Wrap each bar in cling wrap and store. The wrapping is necessary because, in humid weather, it tends to sweat.

Chapter 4: Cold Process Soap Recipes

9. Lime LaCroix Cold Process Soap

Ingredients:

- Swirl Quick Mix- 33 oz.
- Sodium Hydroxide Lye- 4.6 oz.
- Flat Lime LaCroix- 10.9 oz.
- Lime Fragrance Oil- 2.4 oz.
- Blue Slushy Mica
- Kermit Green Mica
- Hydrated Chrome Green Colorant
- Aqua Pearl Mica
- Titanium Dioxide

Instructions:

1. Start by slowly mixing the 4.6 ounces of lye with 10.9 ounces of LaCroix. Allow them to cool down to below 100°F.
2. Take out a pan and melt your Swirl Quick Mix. Don't overheat the oils. Whisk until they are mixed well.
3. Use a thermometer to check the temperature of the oil mixture. Ensure that it is 100°F above the lye solution.
4. While you wait for it to get to the right temperature, mix your Blue Slushy Mica, Kermit Green Mica, Hydrated Chrome Green Colorant, Aqua Pearl Mica and Titanium Dioxide in a bowl. Whisk well.
5. Once the temperatures are right, mix the lye-water with the oil mixture before you add your whisked Titanium Dioxide mixture.

6. Hand-mix it before you use a stick blender to mix it well.
7. After that, add your Lime Fragrance Oil.
8. Put the mixture in the pre-lined mold then spray with 99% isopropyl alcohol to prevent soda ash.
9. Press your blackberry seeds on the soap bars.
10. Refrigerate them for about two days.
11. Immediately after your soap has hardened, remove it from your mold, then cut it.
12. Allow it to cure for at least 4 weeks.

10. Kelly Green Cold Process Soap

Ingredients:

- Basic Quick Mix- 33 oz.
- Distilled Water- 10.9 oz.
- Sodium Hydroxide Lye- 4.7 oz.
- Sodium Lactate- 10 g.
- Apple Sage Fragrance Oil- 2.4 oz.
- Kelly Green Mica- 5 g.

Instructions:

1. Start by slowly mixing the 4.7 ounces of lye with 10.9 ounces of water. Allow them to cool down to below 100°F.
2. Take out a pan and melt your Basic Quick Mix. Don't overheat the oils. Whisk until they are mixed well.
3. Use a thermometer to check the temperature of the oil mixture. Ensure that it is 100°F above the lye solution.
4. While you wait for it to get to the right temperature, mix your Kelly Green Mica in a bowl. Whisk well.
5. Once the temperatures are right, mix the lye-water into the oil mixture before you add your whisked Kelly Green Mica- mixture.
6. Hand-mix it before you use a stick blender to mix it well.
7. After that, add your Apple Sage Fragrance Oil.
8. Put the mixture in the pre-lined mold then spray with 99% isopropyl alcohol to prevent soda ash.
9. Refrigerate them for about two days.

10. Immediately after your soap has hardened, remove it from your mold, then cut it.
11. Allow it to cure for at least 4 weeks.

11. Blue Handmade Cold Process Soap

Ingredients:

- Swirl Quick Mix- 33 oz.
- Distilled Water- 10.9 oz.
- Sodium Hydroxide Lye- 4.6 oz.
- Sodium Lactate- 10 g.
- fragrance oil- 2.4 oz.
- black colorant- 2 g.
- blue colorant- 2.5 g.

Instructions:

1. Start by slowly mixing the 4.6 ounces of lye with 10.9 ounces of water. Allow them to cool down to below 100°F. Add your sodium lactate.
2. Take out a pan and melt your Swirl Quick Mix. Don't overheat the oils. Whisk until they are mixed well.
3. Use a thermometer to check the temperature of the oil mixture. Ensure that it is 100°F above the lye solution.
4. While you wait for it to get to the right temperature, mix your black colorant and blue colorant in a bowl. Whisk well.
5. Once the temperatures are right, mix the lye-water with the oil mixture before you add your whisked black colorant mixture.
6. Hand-mix it before you use a stick blender to mix it well.
7. After that, add your Fragrance Oil.
8. Put the mixture in the pre-lined mold then spray with 99% isopropyl alcohol to prevent soda ash.

9. Refrigerate them for about two days.
10. Immediately after your soap has hardened, remove it from your mold, then cut it.
11. Allow it to cure for at least 4 weeks.

12. Moonstone Cold Process Soap

Ingredients:

- Basic Quick Mix- 54 oz.
- Sodium Hydroxide Lye- 7.7 oz.
- Distilled Water- 15.1 oz.
- Moonstone Fragrance Oil- 3.5 oz.
- Titanium Dioxide
- Snowflake Sparkle Mica
- Aqua Pearl Mica
- Magenta Mica
- Lavender Mica
- Party Pink Mica

Instructions:

1. Start by slowly mixing the 7.7 ounces of lye with 15.1 ounces of water. Allow them to cool down to below 100°F. Add your sodium lactate.
2. Take out a pan and melt your Basic Quick Mix. Don't overheat the oils. Whisk until they are mixed well.
3. Use a thermometer to check the temperature of the oil mixture. Ensure that it is 100°F above the lye solution.
4. While you wait for it to get to the right temperature, mix your Titanium Dioxide, Snowflake Sparkle Mica, Aqua Pearl Mica, Magenta Mica, Lavender Mica and Party Pink Mica in a bowl. Whisk well.
5. Once the temperatures are right, mix the lye-water into the oil mixture before you add your whisked Titanium Dioxide mixture.

6. Hand-mix it before you use a stick blender to mix it well.
7. After that, add your Moonstone Fragrance Oil.
8. Put the mixture in the pre-lined mold then spray with 99% isopropyl alcohol to prevent soda ash.
9. Refrigerate them for about two days.
10. Immediately after your soap has hardened, remove it from your mold, then cut it.
11. Allow it to cure for at least 4 weeks.

13. Kokum Butter Cold Process Soap

Ingredients:

- Castor Oil 0.7 oz.
- Coconut Oil 8.5 oz.
- Kokum Butter 1.7 oz.
- Olive Oil- 23.1 oz
- Sodium Hydroxide Lye- 4.7 oz.
- Distilled Water- 10.3 oz.
- Eucalyptus Essential Oil- 2 oz.
- Titanium Dioxide
- Ground Pumpkin Seeds- 15 g.

Instructions:

1. Start by slowly mixing the 4.7 ounces of lye with 10.3 ounces of water. Allow them to cool down to below 100°F. Add your sodium lactate.
2. Take out a pan and melt your Castor Oil, Coconut Oil, Kokum Butter, and Olive Oil. Don't overheat the oils. Whisk until they are mixed well.
3. Use a thermometer to check the temperature of the oil mixture. Ensure that it is 100°F above the lye solution.
4. While you wait for it to get to the right temperature, mix your Titanium Dioxide in a bowl. Whisk well.
5. Once the temperatures are right, mix the lye-water into the oil mixture before you add your whisked Titanium Dioxide mixture.
6. Hand-mix it before you use a stick blender to mix it well.

7. After that, add your Eucalyptus Essential Oil.
8. Put the mixture in the pre-lined mold then spray with 99% isopropyl alcohol to prevent soda ash.
9. Press your ground pumpkin seeds on the soap bars.
10. Refrigerate them for about two days.
11. Immediately after your soap has hardened, remove it from your mold, then cut it.
12. Allow it to cure for at least 4 weeks.

14. Coffee Cold Process Soap

Ingredients:

- Swirl Recipe Quick Mix- 54 oz.
- Sodium Hydroxide Lye- 7. 5 oz.
- Plain Coffee- 17.8 oz.
- Espresso Fragrance Oil- 3 oz.
- Titanium Dioxide Pigment
- Brown Oxide Pigment
- Black Oxide Pigment
- Used Coffee Grounds- 10 g.
- Whole Espresso Beans (for the top)

Instructions:

1. Start by slowly mixing the 7.5 ounces of lye with 17.8 ounces of water. Allow them to cool down to below 100°F. Add your sodium lactate.
2. Take out a pan and melt your Swirl Recipe Quick Mix. Don't overheat the oils. Whisk until they are mixed well.
3. Use a thermometer to check the temperature of the oil mixture. Ensure that it is 100°F above the lye solution.
4. While you wait for it to get to the right temperature, mix your Titanium Dioxide Pigment, Brown Oxide Pigment, Black Oxide Pigment and Used Coffee Grounds in a bowl. Whisk well.
5. Once the temperatures are right, mix the lye-water into the oil mixture before you add your whisked Titanium Dioxide mixture.

6. Hand-mix it before you use a stick blender to mix it well.
7. After that, add your Espresso Fragrance Oil.
8. Put the mixture in the pre-lined mold then spray with 99% isopropyl alcohol to prevent soda ash.
9. Press your whole espresso beans on the soap bars.
10. Refrigerate them for about two days.
11. Immediately after your soap has hardened, remove it from your mold, then cut it.
12. Allow it to cure for at least 4 weeks.

15. Lavender Kombucha Cold Process Soap

Ingredients:

- Swirl Recipe Quick Mix- 39 oz.
- Sodium Hydroxide Lye 5.5 oz.
- Prepped Kombucha 11.6 oz.
- Lavender Mica
- Titanium Dioxide
- Lavender 40/42 Essential Oil- 2 oz.
- Lavender Buds

Instructions:

1. Start by slowly mixing the 5.5 ounces of lye with 11.6 ounces of Prepped Kombucha. Allow them to cool down to below 100°F. Add your sodium lactate.
2. Take out a pan and melt your Swirl Recipe Quick Mix. Don't overheat the oils. Whisk until they are mixed well.
3. Use a thermometer to check the temperature of the oil mixture. Ensure that it is 100°F above the lye solution.

4. While you wait for it to get to the right temperature, mix your Lavender Mica and
5. Titanium Dioxide in a bowl. Whisk well.
6. Once the temperatures are right, mix the lye-water into the oil mixture before you add your whisked Titanium Dioxide mixture.
7. Hand-mix it before you use a stick blender to mix it well.
8. After that, add your Lavender 40/42 Essential Oil.
9. Put the mixture in the pre-lined mold then spray with 99% isopropyl alcohol to prevent soda ash.
10. Press your Lavender buds on the soap bars.
11. Refrigerate them for about two days.
12. Immediately after your soap has hardened, remove it from your mold, then cut it.
13. Allow it to cure for at least 4 weeks.

16. Zesty Green Cold Process Soap

Ingredients:

- Swirl Quick Mix- 33 oz.
- Sodium Hydroxide Lye- 4.6 oz.
- Distilled Water- 10.9 oz.
- Ginger Lime Fragrance Oil- 1 oz.
- Green Salsa Fragrance Oil- 1 oz.
- Green Chrome Oxide Pigment
- Titanium Dioxide
- Green Forest Jojoba Beads- 15 g.

Instructions:

1. Start by slowly mixing the 4.6 ounces of lye with 10.9 ounces of water. Allow them to cool down to below 100°F. Add your sodium lactate.
2. Take out a pan and melt your Swirl Quick Mix. Don't overheat the oils. Whisk until they are mixed well.
3. Use a thermometer to check the temperature of the oil mixture. Ensure that it is 100°F above the lye solution.
4. While you wait for it to get to the right temperature, mix your Green Chrome Oxide Pigment and Titanium Dioxide in a bowl. Whisk well.
5. Once the temperatures are right, mix the lye-water into the oil mixture before you add your whisked titanium dioxide mixture.
6. Hand-mix it before you use a stick blender to mix it well.

7. After that, add your Ginger Lime Fragrance Oil and Green Salsa Fragrance Oil.
8. Put the mixture in the pre-lined mold then spray with 99% isopropyl alcohol to prevent soda ash.
9. Press your Green Forest Jojoba Beads on the soap bars.
10. Refrigerate them for about two days.
11. Immediately after your soap has hardened, remove it from your mold, then cut it.
12. Allow it to cure for at least 4 weeks.

17. Energizing Orange Cold Process Soap

Ingredients:

- Lots of Lather Quick Mix- 33 oz.
- Distilled Water- 10 oz.
- Sodium Hydroxide Lye- 4.7 oz.
- Sodium Lactate- 10 g.
- 10X Orange Essential Oil- 1.7 oz.
- Orange Peel Powder- 15 g.
- Marigold Petals
- 99% Isopropyl Alcohol in Spray Bottle

Instructions:

1. Start by slowly mixing the 4.7 ounces of lye with 10 ounces of water. Allow them to cool down to below 100°F. Add your sodium lactate.
2. Take out a pan and melt your Lots of Lather Quick Mix. Don't overheat the oils. Whisk until they are mixed well.
3. Use a thermometer to check the temperature of the oil mixture. Ensure that it is 100°F above the lye solution.
4. While you wait for it to get to the right temperature, mix your Orange Peel Powder in a bowl. Whisk well.
5. Once the temperatures are right, mix the lye-water into the oil mixture before you add your whisked Orange Peel Powder mixture.
6. Hand-mix it before you use a stick blender to mix it well.
7. After that, add your 10X Orange Essential Oil.

8. Put the mixture in the pre-lined mold then spray with 99% isopropyl alcohol to prevent soda ash.
9. Press your marigold petals on the soap.
10. Refrigerate them for about two days.
11. Immediately after your soap has hardened, remove it from your mold, then cut it.
12. Allow it to cure for at least 4 weeks.

18. Orange & Clove Spice Cold Process Soap

- Yields: 1 loaf of 3 lbs.

Ingredients

- 45 oz. Olive oil
- 32 oz. Coconut oil
- 8 oz. Castor oil
- 12 oz. Lye
- 32 oz. Distilled water
- 2 oz. Orange fold 5 essential oil
- 8 oz. Clove essential oil
- 2-15 g black walnut powder

Instructions

1. Prepare this soap batter with the normal cold process method as described.
2. Black walnut powder is optional but gives your bar of soap a rustic decoration that compliments the musk fragrance and imitates the appearance of ground clove.
3. Add fragrances and embellishments at the end of the process; pour into your mold and set aside.
4. Cut in 24 – 48 hours. Allow this bar 6 weeks to cure.
5. Remember, soap with a high content of olive oil need a little longer time to cure in order to get a better lather.

19. Honey & Beeswax Soap

- Yields: 1 loaf of 2 lbs.

Ingredients

- 8 oz. Of water
- 4 oz. Of lye
- 10 oz. Of coconut oil
- 2 oz. Of shea butter
- 12 oz. Of olive oil
- 2 oz. Of sweet almond oil
- 2 oz. Of sunflower oil
- 1.5 oz. Honey almond fragrance oil
- 15 g. Of beeswax pastilles
- 15 g. Of local honey

Instructions:

1. Prepare this recipe with the normal cold process method described.
2. Melt the beeswax pastilles completely in the microwave before mixing.
3. If they are not completely liquid, they will not melt into the batter properly.
4. Add the fragrance and honey at the very end. Honey will accelerate the trace.
5. This will give less time to work with the soap before it hardens.

20. Woodland Pine Soap

- Yields: 1 loaf of 2 lbs.

Ingredients

- 8 oz. Of water
- 4.1 oz. Of lye
- 12 oz. Of coconut oil
- 2 oz. Of shea butter
- 10 oz. Of olive oil
- 2 oz. Of hemp oil
- 2 oz. Of soybean oil
- 1.5 oz. Of pine fragrance oil
- green mica
- 2 g of woodland green mica
- 5 g of white pearl mica

Instructions:

1. This soap is very aesthetic with its popping colors. First start this recipe by mixing your bright colors.
2. Take three oz. Of olive oil and separate an ounce into three cups. Mix your micas until a smooth colorant is achieved and set aside.
3. Prepare your soap batter with the basic cold process method. Remember, you will be mixing 7 oz.
4. Of olive oil as you have just removed 3 oz. Once your batter is mixed. Add the fragrance.
5. Separate your batter into three parts and color each part.

6. Pour each color into your mold with a drop swirl technique and give it a twist with your spoon.
7. Set aside to harden for 24 hours before cutting.

21. Sweet Pear Soap

- Yields: 1 loaf of 5 lbs.

Ingredients

- 22 oz. Of olive oil
- 4 oz. Of pureed dessert pears
- 18 oz. Of coconut oil
- 18 oz. Of water
- 8 oz. Of lye
- 8 oz. Of shea butter
- 8 oz. Of avocado oil
- 8 oz. Of rice bran oil
- 4 oz. Of sweet juicy pear fragrance oil
- 2 g. Of lavender mica powder
- 2 g. Of teal mica powder

Instructions:

1. First prepare your pureed pears. Mix them to a soft pulp in a texture like baby food and set aside.
2. In the basic cold process method prepare your lye solution and oils.
3. Mix the two parts when the temperatures both have cooled to about 100 degrees. Mix with your stick blender until a light trace has been reached.
4. Add your pear puree and fragrance and mix thoroughly. Split the batter into two parts and color each part. Mix into your molds with a layered and swirl technique.

5. Give this bar large fat swirls. The fruity smell is a popular fragrance, and the fruit puree creates a smooth texture. Unmold and cut after 24 hours.

22. Lemongrass Swirl

- Yields: 1 loaf of 4 lbs.

Ingredients

- 8 oz. Of water
- 12 oz. Of coconut oil
- 2 oz. Of shea butter
- 2 oz. Of cocoa butter
- 10 oz. Of olive oil
- 2 oz. Of hemp seed oil
- 4.1 oz. Of lye
- 1.5 oz. Of lemongrass oil / fragrance oil
- blue mica
- 20 g of yellow mica

Instructions:

1. Make the batter with the basic cold process technique. This is a small recipe and easy to complete. Mix your lye and oils completely.
2. Add your shea butter at the end of this process. Try to keep your trace light.
3. Add your fragrance and split the batter into two parts. Mix your two colors. One part will have 10 g. Of yellow mica. The other will have 10 g.
4. Of yellow and 2.5 g of blue mics. Pour the yellow part into your mold and then drop the green batter from several inches above allowing the batter to drop into the yellow color.

5. Now swirl with your spoon for those long wispy swirls. This is called the drop swirl technique.
6. Set your mold aside and cut this loaf after 24 hours.

23. Mango Butter With Ylang Ylang

- Yields: 1 loaf of 1 lb.

Ingredients

- 3.2 oz. Of mango butter
- 4.8 oz. Of shea butter
- 8.5 oz. Of coconut oil
- 3 oz. Of avocado oil
- 3 oz. Of castor oil
- 9.5 oz. Of olive oil
- 10.5 oz. Of distilled water
- 4.3 oz. Of lye
- 2 oz. Of ylang essential oil

Instructions:

1. This bar requires the basic instructions from the cold process described. Here our ingredients are focused on the mango and ylang.
2. Allow your mango butter to the last of the oils that are blended. This will allow the super fat to be the mango butter and that will be the moisture that remains untouched by the lye.
3. Ylang is an essential oil. Remember essential oils go a long way, so no more than 2 oz.
4. After mixing your batter you can leave this bar uncolored or you can give it a touch of floral color mica.

5. Ylang-ylangs are yellow, so that would be fitting. Set to harden for 24 hours before cutting, and cure for 4 – 6 weeks.

24. Raw Honey & Dandelion Soap

- Yields: 3 bars

Ingredients

- 14 oz. Of olive oil
- 8 oz. Of coconut oil
- 3 oz. Of sunflower oil
- 2 oz. Of shea butter
- 1.5 oz. Of jojoba oil
- 1.5 oz. Of sweet almond oil
- 10 oz. Of dandelion tea
- 4 oz. Of lye
- 5 oz. Of raw honey

Instructions:

1. First make your tea. The dandelions in this soap aren't special. You can get them straight from the back yard.
2. Wash them and boil them down in a pot of water. You will get a light green water just as you do when you boil spinach.
3. Leave the leaves in the water and let it sit in your fridge overnight.
4. Next make your batter in the normal cold process way. You want your jojoba to be the super fat in this recipe so blend everything well and add the jojoba as the last oil.
5. Add your honey at the end and blend well. Honey can accelerate a batch of soap to a thicker trace more quickly, so only add it when you are ready.

6. Set this into your mold and cut in 24 hours. This recipe will give you a lite honey grass small. Feel free to add additional flower fragrances to tweak it if necessary.

25. Summertime Watermelon Soap

- Yields: 1 loaf of 3 lbs.

Ingredients

- Water 18.24 oz.
- Lye 6.95 oz.
- Canola 9.6 oz.
- Olive 9.6 oz.
- Coconut 16.8 oz.
- Lard 9.6 oz.
- Shea butter 2.4 oz.
- Colorant green, pink, titanium dioxide
- Fragrance watermelon 2.5 oz.
- Black large sprinkles

Instructions:

1. Mix your batter in the standard cold process way. Once your oils and lye are mixed add your fragrance.
2. You will split this batter into three bowls. Most of your batter will be colored pink. Two small bowls will be mixed with green and white separately.
3. The green will be the first layer poured. The white will be the second layer poured. Mix your large black sprinkles into your pink batter before you pour it.
4. Layer the pink on the top. Pour gently so that you do not disrupt the two bottom layers.
5. One way to do this is to pour directly onto spoon to absorb the impact.

6. This way your batter will fall more gently. Set aside and let set for 24 hours before you cut.

26. Vanilla Cupcakes

- Yields: 1200 gcakes

Ingredients

- water 14-ounce lye 7.3 ounces of coconut oil
- 18.5 oz. of fat Vegetable oil (15 oz).
- 11.5 ounces of olive oil Castor oil (15 ounces)
- 7.3 ounces of shea butter
- 2.5 ounces of white colorant titanium dioxide, dark purple mica.
- A scent of black cherries 25 oz.

Instructions:

1. In one basin, mix the oils and lye according to the cold process method.
2. Allow both combinations to cool down. Combine them, pour in your scent, and divide the soap mixture into two portions.
3. Mix well, but do not overmix; you want to give the batter enough time to work with, so leave it at a light trace.
4. Pour the first portion of the mixture into the cupcake holders after mixing the titanium dioxide into the bowl until the color is as near to white or vanilla cake as you wish.
5. Add a dark purple color to one dish of batter. Then divide the batter into two bowls once again.
6. Add titanium dioxide to the batter in the second bowl until it becomes a lighter purple color.

7. Mixing the batter until peaks begin to form will help you get it to a thicker trace. Now fill the two frosting bags with your two tones of purple batter.
8. On each cupcake, pipe a circle of dark frosting. Next, apply a thinner layer of a lighter purple color over the top of the white layer, and then garnish with a dollop of the initial frosting.
9. Give these a full day to harden before rearranging them.

Chapter 5: Hot Process Goat Milk, Green Tea and Citrus Soaps

27. Goat Milk, Green Tea, Lemon and Lavender Soap

- Prep Time: about 50-60 minutes
- Cooking Time: 40 minutes

Ingredients:

- 30 g green tea leaves, ground
- 15 oz green tea oil
- 12 oz lemon essential oil
- 10 oz lavender essential oil
- 18 oz olive oil
- 12 oz palm oil
- 12 oz castor oil
- 5 oz raw shea butter
- 11 oz goat milk
- 8 oz 100% pure lye

How to Make Homemade Soap:

1. Pour the lye into the cold goat milk and mix well until there is a homogenous consistency.
2. In a pot, combine the olive, palm and castor oils. Melt the oils for 10 minutes. Keep stirring to prevent oils from burning. Add in the shea butter and melt with the oils for 10 minutes.
3. Pour the lye and goat milk batter into the oils and mix well. Add the tea leaves.
4. Simmer the lye, tea leaves and oils mixture for about 30 minutes and then set the soap batter to cool.
5. Use a PH test to check if the soap is ready. Ideal values are between 7 and 10.
6. Add the green tea oil, lemon essential oil and lavender essential oil. Beat the ingredients with a blender until there is a smooth consistency.
7. Pour the soap into the molds and use after few weeks.

28. Goat Milk, Green Tea and Lemon Soap

- Prep Time: about 70-80 minutes
- Cooking Time: 60-65 minutes

Ingredients:

- 5 dried lemon slices
- 15 oz green tea oil
- 30 g lemon zest, minced.
- 15 oz olive oil
- 14 oz palm oil
- 15 g vitamin D
- 200 g of goat milk
- 7 oz lye

How to Make Homemade Soap:

1. Spoon the lye into the goat milk mixture and mix well. Spoon the lemon zest and stir well.
2. Cool the mixture in the well-ventilated room.
3. Mix together the olive and palm oils and mix well. Melt the oils over the low heat for 10 minutes. Keep stirring well to prevent the oils from burning.
4. Then slowly pour the lye and goat milk mixture into the oils and mix well.
5. Simmer the lye and oils mixture for about 50 minutes. Keep stirring to prevent the soap batter from burning and rising.
6. Use a PH test to check if the soap is ready. Ideal values are between 7 and 10. If the indicator is higher than 10, then this means that the soap is not ready.

7. Spoon the vitamin D and green tea oil. Blend the soap batter with a stick blender until there is a creamy consistency.
8. Place the dried lemon slices on the bottom of the molds. Then pour the soap batter on top. In 20-24 hours take the soap out of the molds and cut it into bars. Use the soap after two or three weeks when the process of the saponification will complete.

29. Goat Milk, Green Tea and Almond Soap

- Prep Time: 60-65 minutes
- Cooking Time: 55 minutes

Ingredients:

- 25 oz green tea oil
- 18 oz almond oil
- 15 oz coconut oil
- 12 oz olive oil
- 7 oz castor oil
- 15 g vitamin A
- 8-9 oz goat milk
- 8 oz lye

How to Make Homemade Soap:

1. Pour the lye into the cold goat milk and mix well until the creamy mass. Then cool for about 20-30 minutes.
2. In a pot, mix the coconut oil with the olive oil and castor oil. Boil the oils on the burner for around 15 minutes.
3. Pour the lye and goat milk batter into the oils and mix well.
4. Boil the lye and oils mixture over the low heat for about 40 minutes. Then set the soap batter aside to cool it.
5. Use a PH test to check if the soap is ready. The values should stay between 7 and 10.

6. Then pour the green tea oil, sweet almond oil and vitamin A. Blend all the soap ingredients well until there is a creamy and smooth mass.
7. Spoon or ladle the soap into the molds. In 20-24 hours take your soap out of the molds. Wait for three weeks until the process of the saponification will complete and only then use the handmade soap.

30. Goat Milk, Green Tea and Grapefruit Soap

- Prep Time: about 70-80 minutes
- Cooking Time: 60-65 minutes

Ingredients:

- 5 grapefruit slices
- 15 oz green tea oil
- 15 oz grapefruit essential oil
- 15 oz olive oil
- 14 oz palm oil
- 2 oz shea butter
- 15 g vitamin D
- 10 oz goat milk
- 8 oz lye

How to Make Homemade Soap:

1. Spoon the lye into the cold goat milk mixture and mix well.
2. Cool the mixture in the well-ventilated room.
3. Mix together the olive oil, palm oil and shea butter. Mix well. Melt the oils over the low heat for 10 minutes. Keep stirring well to prevent the oils from burning.
4. Then slowly pour the lye and goat milk mixture into the oils and mix well.
5. Simmer the lye and oils mixture for about 50 minutes. Keep stirring to prevent the soap batter from burning and rising.

6. Use a PH test to check if the soap is ready. Ideal values are between 7 and 10. If the indicator is higher than 10, then this means that the soap is not ready.
7. Spoon the vitamin D, grapefruit essential oil and green tea oil. Blend the soap batter with a stick blender until there is a creamy mass.
8. Place the grapefruit slices on the bottom of the molds. Then pour the soap batter on top. In 20-24 hours take the soap out of the molds and cut it into bars. Use the soap after two or three weeks when the process of the saponification will complete.

31. Goat Milk, Green Tea, Honey and Orange Soap

- Prep Time: about 60-70 minutes
- Cooking Time: 50 minutes

Ingredients:

- 20 oz green tea oil
- 15 oz orange essential oil
- 8 oz honey
- 20 oz coconut oil
- 15 oz olive oil
- 12 oz palm oil
- 9-10 oz goat milk
- 8 oz lye

How to Make Homemade Soap:

1. Spoon the lye into the cold goat milk and mix well until there is a homogenous mass. Remember that the fumes will be produced during this process, so don't forget to wear the rubber gloves, goggles and breathing mask. Let it cool for around 20 minutes.
2. In a pot, combine the oils. Melt the oils on a burner 20 minutes and keep stirring.
3. Pour the lye and goat milk batter into the oils and stir well.
4. Cook the lye and oils mixture over the low heat for about 30 minutes. Keep stirring to prevent the soap batter from burning and then cool the soap.
5. Check if the soap is ready using a PH test. Ideal values are between 7 and 10.

6. Mix in the green tea oil, honey and orange essential oil. Mix all the ingredients using a stick blender until there is a homogenous mass.
7. Pour the soap batter into the molds. In 20-24 hours take the soap out of the molds and cut it into bars. Wait for two or three weeks and use the soap.

32. Goat Milk, Green Tea, Orange and Cherry Soap

- Prep Time: about 80-90 minutes
- Cooking Time: 60 minutes

Ingredients:

- 20 oz green tea oil
- 15 g orange zest, minced
- 15 oz orange essential oil
- 15 oz cherry kernel oil
- 14 oz coconut oil
- 14 oz olive oil
- 12 oz palm oil
- 10 oz goat milk
- 8 oz lye

How to Make Homemade Soap:

1. Add the orange zest to the goat milk and mix well to.
2. Spoon the lye into the goat milk with the orange zest and mix well.
3. The fumes will be produced during the lye melting process. Wear the rubber gloves, goggles and breathing mask.
4. Cool for around one or two hours. Place the lye into the well-ventilated room or on the balcony.
5. Mix together the coconut, olive and palm oils and stir well. Melt the oils over the low heat for around 30 minutes. Keep stirring well to prevent them from burning.

6. Then slowly pour the lye and goat milk batter into the oils and mix well.
7. Boil the lye and oils mixture over the low heat for about 30 minutes. Keep stirring to prevent the soap batter from burning and rising. Then cool the soap batter.
8. Use a PH test to check if the soap is ready. Ideal values are between 7 and 10. If the indicator is higher than 10, then this means that the soap is not ready.
9. Add the green tea, cherry kernel and orange essential oils. Blend using a stick blender until there is a creamy mass.
10. Pour the soap batter into the molds. In 20-24 hours take the soap out of the molds and cut it into pieces. You can use the soap after two or three weeks.

33. Goat Milk, Green Tea, Lemon and Peach Soap

- Prep Time: about 90 minutes
- Cooking Time: 80 minutes

Ingredients:

- 20 oz green tea oil
- 15 g lemon zest, minced
- 15 oz lemon essential oil
- 15 oz peach essential oil
- 14 oz coconut oil
- 12 oz olive oil
- 10 oz palm oil
- 8 oz goat milk
- 7 oz lye

How to Make Homemade Soap:

1. Pour the lye into the goat milk and mix well.
2. The fumes will be produced during the lye melting process. Wear the rubber gloves, goggles and breathing mask.
3. Cool for around one or two hours. Place the lye into the well-ventilated room or on the balcony.
4. Mix together the coconut, olive and palm oils and stir well. Melt the oils over the low heat for around 30 minutes. Keep stirring well to prevent them from burning.
5. Then slowly pour the lye and goat milk mixture into the oils and mix well.

6. Boil the lye and oils mixture over the low heat for about 45-50 minutes. Keep stirring to prevent the soap batter from burning and rising. Then cool the soap batter.
7. Use a PH test to check if the soap is ready. Ideal values are between 7 and 10. If the indicator is higher than 10, then this means that the soap is not ready.
8. Mix in the lemon zest, green tea oil, lemon essential oil and peach essential oil. Stir or blend well.
9. Ladle the soap batter into the molds. You can use the soap after two or three weeks.

34. Goat Milk, Orange and Blueberry Soap

- Prep Time: about 70-80 minutes
- Cooking Time: 60-65 minutes

Ingredients:

- 20 oz orange essential oil
- 200 g of fresh blueberries
- 20 oz olive oil
- 18 oz palm oil
- 12 oz castor oil
- 8 oz shea butter
- 2 drops blue soap colorant
- 10 oz goat milk
- 8 oz lye

How to Make Homemade Soap:

1. Blend the blueberries with a stick blender. Then cook them over the low heat for 20 minutes. Skim the foam. Keep stirring to prevent blueberries from burning and rising.
2. Spoon the lye into the goat milk and mix well until there is a smooth consistency.
3. Mix together the oils. Then add the shea butter and melt the oils and butter over the low heat for 20 minutes.
4. Put on a mask, rubber gloves and goggles and slowly pour the lye into the oils and mix well.

5. Mix in the blue soap colorant into the lye and oils mixture and blend using a stick blender until there is a pureed mass.
6. Melt the lye and oils mixture over the medium heat for about 30 minutes. Keep stirring to prevent the soap batter from burning and rising.
7. Use a PH test to check if the soap is ready. Ideal values are between 7 and 10. If higher than 10, then cook for 10 minutes and check once more time.
8. Spoon the blueberries and orange essential oil and blend the ingredients well until the pureed consistency.
9. Spoon the soap batter into the square molds. Use the soap after two weeks.

35. Goat Milk, Lemon and Cinnamon Soap

- Prep Time: about 70 minutes
- Cooking Time: 60 minutes

Ingredients:

- 20 oz lemon essential oil
- 10 oz cinnamon essential oil
- 16 oz olive oil
- 15 oz palm oil
- 10 oz castor oil
- 5 oz shea butter
- 10 oz goat milk
- 8 oz lye

How to Make Homemade Soap:

1. Spoon the lye into the cold goat milk and mix well until there is a homogenous mass. Cool for around 30 minutes.
2. Mix together the olive, palm and castor oils. Melt the oils on a burner for around 20 minutes. Then, spoon the shea butter and stir well.
3. Pour the lye and goat milk mixture into the oils and blend using a stick blender until there is a homogenous and pureed mass.
4. Boil over the low heat for about 40 minutes. Keep stirring to prevent the soap batter from burning and rising. Then cool the soap batter.

5. Use a PH test to check if the soap is ready. Ideal values are between 7 and 10. If the indicator is higher than 10, then cook further.
6. Pour the lemon essential oil and cinnamon essential oil. Mix the oils and lye. Use a stick blender or food processor and blend until creamy mass.
7. Pour the soap batter into the molds. In 20-24 hours take the soap out of the molds and cut it into pieces. Then wait and start using the soap.

36. Goat Milk, Grapefruit, Peach and Cinnamon Soap

- Prep Time: about 70 minutes
- Cooking Time: 60 minutes

Ingredients:

- 20 oz grapefruit essential oil
- 15 oz peach essential oil
- 10 oz cinnamon essential oil
- 16 oz olive oil
- 15 oz palm oil
- 8 oz castor oil
- 4 oz cocoa butter
- 10 oz goat milk
- 8-9 oz lye

How to Make Homemade Soap:

1. Spoon the lye into the cold goat milk and mix well until there is a smooth consistency. Cool for around 30 minutes.
2. Mix together the olive, palm and castor oils. Melt the oils on a burner for around 20 minutes. Spoon the cocoa butter and stir well.
3. Pour the lye and goat milk mixture into the oils and blend using a stick blender until there is a creamy mass.
4. Boil over the low heat for about 40 minutes. Keep stirring to prevent the soap batter from burning and rising. Then cool the soap batter.

5. Use a PH test to check if the soap is ready. Ideal values are between 7 and 10. If the indicator is higher than 10, then cook further.
6. Pour the grapefruit essential oil, peach essential oil and cinnamon essential oil. Mix the oils and lye well. You can use a stick blender or a food processor.
7. Pour the soap batter into the molds. In 20-24 hours take the soap out of the molds and cut it into pieces. Then wait for a week or two and start using the soap.

37. Goat Milk, Orange and Olive Soap for Sensitive Skin

- Prep Time: about 50 minutes
- Cooking Time: 20 minutes

Ingredients:

- 20 oz orange essential oil
- 20 oz olive oil
- 13 oz palm oil
- 7 oz castor oil
- 5 oz shea butter
- 12 oz goat milk
- 9 oz lye

How to Make Homemade Soap:

1. Pour the lye into the goat milk and stir well. Cool for around half an hour. Place the mixture into the well-ventilated room or on the balcony.
2. In a pot, combine the olive oil with the palm oil and castor oil. Boil the oils on the burner for around 20 minutes and spoon the shea butter. Cook for 10 minutes or longer until the shea butter melts. Stir all the time.
3. Pour the lye and goat milk mixture into the oils and mix well.
4. Boil the lye and oils mixture over the low heat for about 40 minutes.
5. Cool the batter and check if the soap is ready by using a PH test. The values should stay between 7 and 10.
6. Pour the orange essential oil and blend well.

7. After positive PH test pour the soap batter into the molds. In 20-24 hours take the soap out of the molds and cut it into pieces. Wait for two or three weeks until the process of the saponification will complete and only then use the soap.

Chapter 6: Hand Milling Recipes

Safety precaution

The Hand-milling method does not require you to handle lye. However, if you involve your kids in making hand-milled soaps, you will need to be extra watchful when melting and mixing the soap, because the soap will be hot when heated.

Step 1: prep ahead

Make ready any ingredient that is needed in a particular recipe, get your essential oils, colorants, herbs and other additives ready. Gather all necessary equipment, so that they are within reach when needed. If using a mold that needs lining, line the mold with parchment paper now, so that you are good to go when it is needed.

Hand-milling is similar to melt-and-pour; in that you can avoid working with lye if you make use of a soap base. You can use cold process soaps that don't have additives like coloring and fragrances, or use melt-and-pour soap bases. Alternatively, you can make your own cold-process soap without adding additives like scents and coloring, then allow to saponify for about 24 – 48 hours before hand-milling.

Step 2: measure out all the ingredients

Weigh the soap base, shred it using an electric grater or a hand grater, and then weigh the shredded soap again. Weigh the essential oils in a glass container and set aside. Weigh other additives used in the recipe, if needed; disperse the powdered colorants and additives in 99% isopropyl alcohol. Add the weighed powdered additives into a small cup, add about twice that amount of alcohol into the cup and mix thoroughly.

Step 3: add water to the soap

Add the soap shreds into a slow cooker or double boiler, and then add water to the shreds. It is vital that you add just the right amount of water to the soap, using too little water will cause the soap to be thick and clumpy and may result in dry and flaky soap. On the other hand, using excess water can cause the soap to be more fluid and smoother, and may require more time for the soap to fully cure; also, as the water evaporates during curing it may cause the soap to warp.

Adding 30 g of water per pound of soap shreds is recommended by most accomplished soap crafters, (which is also what I follow). However, this rule is not set in stone, you can add more or less water to your batch depending on the kind of soap you want to make. Moreover, if your soap base is still fresh and has not cured you can add less water; and also add more water if the soap is old and has cured for more than two weeks.

Step 4: melt the soap

Cover the slow cooker and set the heat to low. Stirring occasionally, allow the soap shreds to melt. Turn off the heat when the soap shreds turn lumpy and translucent, with a consistency of mashed potatoes. If you added more water the soap will be more fluid; if you added less water the soap will be thicker.

Step 5: add the additives

After turning off the heat, as the soap cools it will begin to harden and become less fluid; so add any essential oil, colorant or additive required in the recipe quickly and gently mix while the soap is still warm and fluid. Stir the dispersed powdered additives in the measuring cup again before adding into the soap.

Step 6: add to mold

After all the fragrance oils, colorants and additives have been thoroughly mixed into the soap, start scooping the soap into your mold and set aside to let the soap cool and harden. The soap should be hard enough and easily unmolded after about 24 hours.

Step 7: clean your work area

Lye is not used in the hand-milling soap making process, this makes it easy to clean up. You can use regular dishwashing detergent and hot water to clean your equipment.

Step 8: unmold the soap

Remove the soap from the mold once it is hard enough, if the soap is still soft and sticky allow to stay for another 12 hours and then try unmolding again.

Step 9: cut into bars and cure

After unmolding, cut the soap into bars. Set aside in a cool and dry area, allow to cure for at least one week; this will make the soap milder, harder and last longer as the water in the soap evaporates during curing.

Hand-Milling Soapmaking Issues & Possible Solutions

There are some common issues that will likely come up as you start making hand milled soaps, especially if you are just beginning. Some of these likely problems are listed below, followed by the best possible solution to each issue.

Soap is Difficult to Unmold

Solution: Occasionally, the soap might stick to the sides of the mold, making it difficult to unmold the soap. This occurs in hand-milled soap when too much water is added to the soap. If you experience any difficulty unmolding your soap after 24 hours, allow it to stay for another 12 hours and try unmolding again.

If the soap is still hard to unmold after the extra 12 hours you can place the mold in the freezer for an hour, then try to unmold. If the soap is still stuck, put it back in the freezer for another 30 minutes and then try again.

Oil Leaks from the Soap

Solution: If fragrance oil or essential oil leaks out of the finished soap bar, this usually indicates that they were not properly mixed with the soap base. Soap batches that exhibit this are actually okay to be used as is, however, to remedy this, melt the soap and mix thoroughly before pouring it back into the mold.

Color Patches in the Soap

Solution: This usually occurs when powdered colorants are added directly to the soap base, this causes the powder to clump when the mixture is stirred. To prevent this, first disperse the powdered colorants in 99% isopropyl alcohol, ensure you mix well before adding into the soap base.

The Soap is Hard and Dry at the Sides

Solution: If the soap dries out and cakes at the sides in the slow cooker, this is usually an indication that the heat is too high. You can spoon out the soap in the middle that is still fluid, to separate it from the dried soap at the sides, and then continue with the recipe using the scooped-out fluid soap.

Alternatively, you can scrape the dried soap from the sides and mix together with the fluid soap in the middle, then add 15 g of water and mix them thoroughly. This will help remedy the batch, but will yield a soap that is rustic in appearance and rough in texture.

38. Geranium Clay Soap

- Yield: 2 pounds
- Scent: geranium and peppermint
- Total time: 1 to 2 hours (melting, mixing and pouring), 24 hours in the mold, 1 to 2 weeks for curing.

Equipment:

- Soap mold
- Double boiler
- Infrared thermometer
- Digital scale
- Hand/cheese grater
- Measuring cups
- Measuring spoons
- Silicone spatula
- Stainless steel spoon
- Hand whisk

Ingredients:

Scent:

- 0.3 ounces peppermint essential oil
- 0.4 ounces geranium essential oil

Rebatch Soap Base:

- 2 pounds unscented and uncolored soap base
- 50 ml water

Colorants/Additives:

- 10 g orange Moroccan clay powder
- 1½ tbsp isopropyl alcohol

Directions:

1. Add the isopropyl alcohol in a measuring cup, add the Moroccan clay powder and stir well to disperse. Weigh the essential oils into a glass cup, mix well to blend the oils. Measure out the needed amount of soap base, then shred the soap using a hand/cheese grater.
2. Place a double boiler in the stove, set the heat to medium-low, add the soap shreds into the double boiler, then add the aloe vera gel. Gently stir the soap base at regular intervals until it fully melts, then turn off the heat. (If the soap base seems to be drying out you can add more water to wet it)
3. After turning off the heat you will need to work quickly, because as the soap cools down it will start to harden and dry out. Add the essential oils and the dispersed Moroccan clay powder to the melted soap base, stir well to allow it blend in.
4. Spoon the soap into the mold, you can smoothen the surface of the soap in the mold with a spatula.
5. Set the mold aside for about 24 – 48 hours to allow the soap to harden. When the soap is hard enough, remove from the mold, cut into bars if a loaf mold was used.
6. Place the soap bars in a cool and dry area, allow them to cure for about 1 – 2 weeks.

39. Chocolate Oatmeal Soap

- Scent: geranium and eucalyptus
- Total time: 1 to 2 hours (melting, mixing and pouring), 24 hours in the mold, 1 to 2 weeks for curing.

Equipment:

- Soap mold
- Double boiler
- Infrared thermometer
- Digital scale
- Hand/cheese grater
- Measuring cups
- Measuring spoons
- Silicone spatula
- Stainless steel spoon
- Hand whisk

Ingredients:

Scent:

- 0.4 ounces geranium essential oil
- 0.3 ounces eucalyptus essential oil

Rebatch Soap Base:

- 2 pounds unscented and uncolored soap base
- 50 ml of water

Colorants/Additives:

- 10 g finely ground oats
- 10 g isopropyl alcohol
- 5 g unsweetened cocoa powder

Directions:

1. Add the isopropyl alcohol in a measuring cup, add the cocoa powder and stir well to disperse. Weigh the essential oils into a glass cup, mix well to blend the oils. Measure out the needed amount of soap base, then shred the soap using a hand/cheese grater.
2. Place a double boiler in the stove, set the heat to medium-low, add the soap shreds into the double boiler, then add water. Gently stir the soap base at regular intervals until it fully melts, then turn off the heat. (If the soap base seems to be drying out you can add more water to wet it)
3. After turning off the heat you will need to work quickly, because as the soap cools down it will start to harden and dry out. Add the essential oils, the ground oats and cocoa powder to the melted soap base, stir well to allow it blend in.

4. Spoon the soap into the mold, you can smoothen the surface of the soap in the mold with a spatula.
5. Set the mold aside for about 24 – 48 hours to allow the soap to harden. When the soap is hard enough, remove from the mold, cut into bars if a loaf mold was used.
6. Place the soap bars in a cool and dry area, allow them to cure for about 1 – 2 weeks.

40. Spearmint Charcoal Soap

Yield: 2 pounds

Scent: rosemary and spearmint

Total time: 1 to 2 hours (melting, mixing and pouring), 24 hours in the mold, 1 to 3 weeks for curing.

Equipment:

- Soap mold
- Double boiler
- Infrared thermometer
- Digital scale
- Hand/cheese grater
- Measuring cups
- Measuring spoons
- Silicone spatula
- Stainless steel spoon
- Hand whisk

Ingredients:

Scent:

- 0.4 ounces rosemary essential oil
- 0.3 ounces spearmint essential oil

Rebatch Soap Base:

- 2 pounds unscented and uncolored soap base
- 50 ml water

Colorants/Additives:

- 10 g activated charcoal powder
- 1½ tbsp isopropyl alcohol

Directions:

1. Add the isopropyl alcohol in a measuring cup, add the charcoal powder and stir well to disperse. Weigh the essential oils into a glass cup, mix well to blend the oils. Measure out the needed amount of soap base, shred the soap using a hand/cheese grater.
2. Place a double boiler in the stove, set the heat to medium-low, add the soap shreds into the double boiler, then add water. Gently stir the soap base at regular intervals until it fully melts, then turn off the heat. (If the soap base seems to be drying out you can add more water to wet it)
3. After turning off the heat you will need to work quickly, because as the soap cools down it will start to harden and dry out. Add the essential oils and the dispersed charcoal powder to the melted soap base, stir well to allow it blend in.
4. Spoon the soap into the mold, you can smoothen the surface of the soap in the mold with a spatula.
5. Set the mold aside for about 24 – 48 hours to allow the soap to harden. When the soap is hard enough, remove from the mold, cut into bars if a loaf mold was used.
6. Place the soap bars in a cool and dry area, allow them to cure for about 1 – 2 weeks.

41. Orange Rose Soap

- Yield: 2 pounds
- Scent: orange and geranium
- Total time: 1 to 2 hours (melting, mixing and pouring), 24 hours in the mold, 1 to 2 weeks for curing.

Equipment:

- Soap mold
- Double boiler
- Infrared thermometer
- Digital scale
- Hand/cheese grater
- Measuring cups
- Measuring spoons
- Silicone spatula
- Stainless steel spoon
- Hand whisk

INGREDIENTS:

Scent:

- 0.4 ounces orange essential oil
- 0.3 ounces geranium essential oil

Rebatch Soap Base:

- 2 pounds unscented and uncolored soap base
- 50 ml of water

Colorants/Additives:

- 10 g rose clay powder
- 1½ tbsp isopropyl alcohol

Directions:

1. Add the isopropyl alcohol in a measuring cup, add the rose clay powder and stir well to disperse. Weigh the essential oils into a glass cup, mix well to blend the oils. Measure out the needed amount of soap base, then shred the soap using a hand/cheese grater.
2. Place a double boiler in the stove, set the heat to medium-low, add the soap shreds into the double boiler, then add water. Gently stir the soap base at regular intervals until it fully melts, then turn off the heat. (If the soap base seems to be drying out you can add more water to wet it)
3. After turning off the heat you will need to work quickly, because as the soap cools down it will start to harden and dry out. Add the essential oils and the

dispersed rose clay powder to the melted soap base, stir well to allow it blend in.
4. Spoon the soap into the mold, you can smoothen the surface of the soap in the mold with a spatula.
5. Set the mold aside for about 24 – 48 hours to allow the soap to harden. When the soap is hard enough, remove from the mold, cut into bars if a loaf mold was used.
6. Place the soap bars in a cool and dry area, allow them to cure for about 1 – 2 weeks.

42. Oats & Cedarwood Soap

Yield: 2 pounds

Scent: grapefruit, cedarwood and lemongrass

Total time: 1 to 2 hours

Equipment:

- Soap mold
- Double boiler
- Infrared thermometer
- Digital scale
- Hand/cheese grater
- Measuring cups
- Measuring spoons
- Silicone spatula
- Stainless steel spoon
- Hand whisk

Ingredients:

Scent:

- 0.3 ounces grapefruit essential oil
- 0.3 ounces cedarwood essential oil
- 0.2 ounces lemongrass essential oil

Rebatch Soap Base:

- 2 pounds unscented and uncolored soap base
- 50 ml of water

Colorants/Additives:

- 5 g ground coffee powder
- 10 g 99% isopropyl alcohol
- 10 g ground oats

DIRECTIONS:

1. Add 2 teaspoons of isopropyl alcohol in a measuring cup, add the coffee powder and stir well to disperse. Weigh the essential oils into a glass cup, mix well to blend the oils. Measure out the needed amount of soap base, then shred the soap using a hand/cheese grater.
2. Place a double boiler in the stove, set the heat to medium-low, add the soap shreds into the double boiler, then add water. Gently stir the soap base at regular intervals until it fully melts, then turn off the heat. (If the soap base seems to be drying out you can add more water to wet it)
3. After turning off the heat you will need to work quickly, because as the soap cools down it will start to harden and dry out. Add the essential oils, the dispersed coffee powder and the ground oats to the melted soap base, stir well to allow it blend in.
4. Spoon the soap into the mold, you can smoothen the surface of the soap in the mold with a spatula.
5. Set the mold aside for about 24 – 48 hours to allow the soap to harden. When the soap is hard enough, remove from the mold, cut into bars if a loaf mold was used.
6. **6:** Place the soap bars in a cool and dry area, allow them to cure for about 1 – 2 weeks.

43. Nettle Leaf & Lavender Soap

Yield: 2 pounds

Scent: lavender and eucalyptus

Total time: 1 to 2 hours 24 hours in the mold, 1 to 2 weeks for curing.

Equipment:

- Soap mold
- Double boiler
- Infrared thermometer
- Digital scale
- Hand/cheese grater
- Measuring cups
- Measuring spoons
- Silicone spatula
- Stainless steel spoon
- Hand whisk

INGREDIENTS:

Scent:

- 0.4 ounces lavender essential oil
- 0.3 ounces eucalyptus essential oil

Rebatch Soap Base:

- 2 pounds unscented and uncolored soap base
- 50 ml of water

Colorants/Additives:

- 10 g nettle leaf powder
- 1½ tbsp isopropyl alcohol

Directions:

1. Add the isopropyl alcohol in a measuring cup, add the nettle powder and stir well to disperse. Weigh the essential oils into a glass cup, mix well to blend the oils. Measure out the needed amount of soap base, then shred the soap using a hand/cheese grater.
2. Place a double boiler in the stove, set the heat to medium-low, add the soap shreds into the double boiler, then add water. Gently stir the soap base at regular intervals until it fully melts, then turn off the heat. (If the soap base seems to be drying out you can add more water to wet it)
3. After turning off the heat you will need to work quickly, because as the soap cools down it will start to harden and dry out. Add the essential oils and the dispersed nettle powder to the melted soap base, stir well to allow it blend in.
4. Spoon the soap into the mold, you can smoothen the surface of the soap in the mold with a spatula.
5. Set the mold aside for about 24 – 48 hours to allow the soap to harden. When the soap is hard enough, remove from the mold, cut into bars if a loaf mold was used.
6. Place the soap bars in a cool and dry area, allow them to cure for about 1 – 2 weeks.

44. Patchouli Bergamot Soap

Yield: 2 pounds

Scent: bergamot and patchouli

Total time: 1 to 2 hours 24 hours in the mold, 1 to 2 weeks for curing.

Equipment:

- Soap mold
- Double boiler
- Infrared thermometer
- Digital scale
- Hand/cheese grater
- Measuring cups
- Measuring spoons
- Silicone spatula
- Stainless steel spoon
- Hand whisk

Ingredients:

Scent:

- 0.4 ounces bergamot essential oil
- 0.3 ounces patchouli essential oil

Rebatch Soap Base:

- 2 pounds unscented and uncolored soap base
- 50 ml water

Colorants/Additives:

- 5 g alkanet root powder
- 5 g poppy seeds
- 10 g isopropyl alcohol

Directions:

1. Add the isopropyl alcohol in a measuring cup, add the alkanet root powder and stir well to disperse. Weigh the essential oils into a glass cup, mix well to blend the oils. Measure out the needed amount of soap base, then shred the soap using a hand/cheese grater.
2. Place a double boiler in the stove, set the heat to medium-low, add the soap shreds into the double boiler, then add water. Gently stir the soap base at regular intervals until it fully melts, then turn off the heat. (If the soap base seems to be drying out you can add more water to wet it)
3. After turning off the heat you will need to work quickly, because as the soap cools down it will start to harden and dry out. Add the essential oils, the dispersed alkanet powder and the poppy seeds to the melted soap base, stir well to allow it blend in.
4. Spoon the soap into the mold, you can smoothen the surface of the soap in the mold with a spatula.
5. Set the mold aside for about 24 – 48 hours to allow the soap to harden. When the soap is hard enough, remove from the mold, cut into bars if a loaf mold was used.
6. Place the soap bars in a cool and dry area, allow them to cure for about 1 – 2 weeks.

45. Eucalyptus Cornmeal Soap

Yield: 2 pounds

Scent: lemon and eucalyptus

Total time: 1 to 2 hours 24 hours in the mold, 1 to 3 weeks for curing.

Equipment:

- Soap mold
- Double boiler
- Infrared thermometer
- Digital scale
- Hand/cheese grater
- Measuring cups
- Measuring spoons
- Silicone spatula
- Stainless steel spoon
- Hand whisk

Ingredients:

Scent:

- 0.4 ounces lemon essential oil
- 0.3 ounces eucalyptus essential oil

Rebatch Soap Base:

- 2 pounds unscented and uncolored soap base
- 50 ml of water

Colorants/Additives:

- 10 g turmeric powder
- 1½ tbsp 99% isopropyl alcohol
- 5 g ground cornmeal

Directions:

1. Add the isopropyl alcohol in a measuring cup, add the turmeric powder and stir well to disperse. Weigh the essential oils into a glass cup, mix well to blend the oils. Measure out the needed amount of soap base, then shred the soap using a hand/cheese grater.
2. Place a double boiler in the stove, set the heat to medium-low, add the soap shreds into the double boiler, then add water. Gently stir the soap base at regular intervals until it fully melts, then turn off the heat. (If the soap base seems to be drying out you can add more water to wet it)
3. After turning off the heat you will need to work quickly, because as the soap cools down it will start to harden and dry out. Add the essential oils, the dispersed rose clay powder and the cornmeal powder to the melted soap base, stir well to allow it blend in.
4. Spoon the soap into the mold, you can smoothen the surface of the soap in the mold with a spatula.
5. Set the mold aside for about 24 – 48 hours to allow the soap to harden. When the soap is hard enough, remove from the mold, cut into bars if a loaf mold was used.
6. Place the soap bars in a cool and dry area, allow them to cure for about 1 – 2 weeks.

46. Oatmeal & Lemon Soap

Yield: 2 pounds

Scent: eucalyptus, lemon and lavender

Total time: 1 to 2 hours (melting, mixing and pouring), 24 hours in the mold, 1 to 2 weeks for curing.

Equipment:

- Soap mold
- Double boiler
- Infrared thermometer
- Digital scale
- Hand/cheese grater
- Measuring cups
- Measuring spoons
- Silicone spatula
- Stainless steel spoon
- Hand whisk

Ingredients:

Scent:

- 0.3 ounces eucalyptus essential oil
- 0.2 ounces lemon essential oil
- 0.2 ounces lavender essential oil

Rebatch Soap Base:

- 2 pounds unscented and uncolored soap base
- 50 ml water

Colorants/Additives:

- 15 gp ground oats
- 10 g turmeric powder
- 1½ tbsp isopropyl alcohol

Directions:

1. Add the isopropyl alcohol in a measuring cup, add the turmeric powder and stir well to disperse.
2. Weigh the essential oils into a glass cup, mix well to blend the oils. Measure out the needed amount of soap base, then shred the soap using a hand/cheese grater.
3. Place a double boiler in the stove, set the heat to medium-low, add the soap shreds into the double boiler, then add water.
4. Gently stir the soap base at regular intervals until it fully melts, then turn off the heat. (If the soap base seems to be drying out you can add more water to wet it)
5. After turning off the heat you will need to work quickly, because as the soap cools down it will start to harden and dry out. Add the essential oils, the ground oats and the dispersed turmeric powder to the melted soap base, stir well to allow it blend in.
6. Spoon the soap into the mold, you can smoothen the surface of the soap in the mold with a spatula.
7. Set the mold aside for about 24 – 48 hours to allow the soap to harden. When the soap is hard enough, remove from the mold, cut into bars if a loaf mold was used.
8. Place the soap bars in a cool and dry area, allow them to cure for about 1 – 2 weeks.

47. Nourishing Lemon Soap

- Yield: 2 pounds
- Scent: geranium, lemon and lemongrass
- Total time: 1 to 2 hours 24 hours in the mold, 1 to 2 weeks for curing.

Equipment:

- Soap mold
- Double boiler
- Infrared thermometer
- Digital scale
- Hand/cheese grater
- Measuring cups
- Measuring spoons
- Silicone spatula
- Stainless steel spoon
- Hand whisk

Ingredients:

Scent:

- 0.4 ounces geranium essential oil
- 0.2 ounces lemongrass essential oil
- 0.2 ounces lemon essential oil

Rebatch Soap Base:

- 2 pounds unscented and uncolored soap base
- 50 ml water

Colorants/Additives:

- 5 g turmeric powder
- 5 g rose clay powder
- 10 g isopropyl alcohol

Directions:

1. Add 15 g of isopropyl alcohol in a measuring cup, add the turmeric powder and stir well to disperse. Add 15 g of isopropyl alcohol in another cup, add the rose clay and stir well to disperse.
2. Weigh the essential oils into a glass cup, mix well to blend the oils. Measure out the needed amount of soap base, then shred the soap using a hand/cheese grater.
3. Place a double boiler in the stove, set the heat to medium-low, add the soap shreds into the double boiler, then add water. Gently stir the soap base at regular intervals until it fully melts, then turn off the heat. (If the soap base seems to be drying out you can add more water to wet it).
4. After turning off the heat you will need to work quickly, because as the soap cools down it will start to harden and dry out. Add the essential oils to the melted soap base, stir well to allow it blend in.
5. Working quickly, spoon half of the soap to a container, add the dispersed turmeric powder to the soap in the container, stir well to blend it in. Add the dispersed rose clay to the remaining half of the soap in the boiler, stir well to blend it in.

6. Spoon the rose colored soap into the mold, smoothen the surface of the soap in the mold with a spatula. Then spoon the turmeric colored soap on the first layer in the mold, smoothen the surface with a spatula.
7. Set the mold aside for about 24 – 48 hours to allow the soap to harden. When the soap is hard enough, remove from the mold and cut into bars.
8. Place the soap bars in a cool and dry area, allow them to cure for about 1 – 2 weeks.

48. Refreshing Rosemary Soap

Yield: 2 pounds

Scent: rosemary, eucalyptus, and spearmint

Total time: 1 to 2 hours 24 hours in the mold, 1 to 2 weeks for curing.

Equipment:

- Soap mold
- Double boiler
- Infrared thermometer
- Digital scale
- Hand/cheese grater
- Measuring cups
- Measuring spoons
- Silicone spatula
- Stainless steel spoon
- Hand whisk

Ingredients:

Scent:

- 0.3 ounces rosemary essential oil
- 0.3 ounces eucalyptus essential oil
- 0.2 ounces spearmint essential oil

Rebatch Soap Base:

- 2 pounds unscented and uncolored soap base
- 50 ml water

Colorants/Additives:

- 10 g orange Moroccan clay powder
- 5 g alkanet root powder
- 15 g isopropyl alcohol

Directions:

1. Add 30 g of isopropyl alcohol in a measuring cup, add the Moroccan clay and stir well to disperse. Add 15 g of isopropyl alcohol in another cup, add the alkanet root powder and stir well to disperse.
2. Weigh the essential oils into a glass cup, mix well to blend the oils. Measure out the needed amount of soap base, then shred the soap using a hand/cheese grater.
3. Place a double boiler in the stove, set the heat to medium-low, add the soap shreds into the double boiler, then add water. Gently stir the soap base at regular intervals until it fully melts, then turn off the heat. (If the soap base seems to be drying out you can add more water to wet it).
4. After turning off the heat you will need to work quickly, because as the soap cools down it will start to harden and dry out. Add the essential oils to the melted soap base, stir well to allow it blend in.
5. Working quickly, spoon half of the soap to a container, add the dispersed alkanet powder to the soap in the container, stir well to blend it in. Add the dispersed Moroccan clay to the remaining half of the soap in the boiler, stir well to blend it in.
6. Spoon the alkanet colored soap into the mold, smoothen the surface of the soap in the mold with a spatula. Then spoon the Moroccan clay colored soap

on the first layer in the mold, smoothen the surface with a spatula.
7. Set the mold aside for about 24 – 48 hours to allow the soap to harden. When the soap is hard enough, remove from the mold and cut into bars.
8. Place the soap bars in a cool and dry area, allow them to cure for about 1 – 2 weeks.

49. Yogurt Coffee Soap

Yield: 2 pounds

Scent: grapefruit and lemongrass

Total time: 1 to 2 hours 24 hours in the mold, 1 to 2 weeks for curing.

Equipment:

- Soap mold
- Double boiler
- Infrared thermometer
- Digital scale
- Hand/cheese grater
- Measuring cups
- Measuring spoons
- Silicone spatula
- Stainless steel spoon
- Hand whisk

Ingredients:

Scent:

- 0.3 ounces lemongrass essential oil
- 0.4 ounces grapefruit essential oil

Rebatch Soap Base:

- 2 pounds unscented and uncolored soap base
- 100 ml plain yogurt

Colorants/Additives:

- 10 g ground coffee powder
- 20 ml isopropyl alcohol

Directions:

1. Add the isopropyl alcohol in a measuring cup, add the ground coffee powder and stir well to disperse. Weigh the essential oils into a glass cup, mix well to blend the oils. Measure out the needed amount of soap base, then shred the soap using a hand/cheese grater.
2. Place a double boiler in the stove, set the heat to medium-low, add the soap shreds into the double boiler, then add the yogurt. Gently stir the soap base at regular intervals until it fully melts, then turn off the heat. (If the soap base seems to be drying out you can add more water to wet it)
3. After turning off the heat you will need to work quickly, because as the soap cools down it will start to harden and dry out. Add the essential oils and the dispersed coffee powder to the melted soap base, stir well to allow it blend in.
4. Spoon the soap into the mold, you can smoothen the surface of the soap in the mold with a spatula.
5. Set the mold aside for about 24 – 48 hours to allow the soap to harden. When the soap is hard enough, remove from the mold, cut into bars if a loaf mold was used.
6. Place the soap bars in a cool and dry area, allow them to cure for about 1 – 2 weeks.

Chapter 7: Liquid Soap Recipes

50. Moisturizing Antibacterial Soap

Ingredients and equipment:

- Liquid castile soap, as required.
- Distilled water or boiled water, as required.
- 30 g vegetable glycerin
- 4 tablespoons almond oil
- 30 drops lavender oil
- 20 drops tea tree oil
- 20 drops cedarwood oil
- 16 ounces pump bottle

Directions:

1. First, pour enough Castile oil to fill the pump bottle up to ½ the bottle.
2. Next, pour almond oil followed by glycerin. Next, add the essential oils.
3. Now pour enough water to fill the bottle, up to 1 inch below the neck of the bottle.

4. Fasten the cap and shake the bottle until well combined.

51. Liquid Hand Soap with Fragrance Variations

Ingredients and equipment:

For soap:

- 100 ml liquid castile soap
- 300 ml distilled water
- 30 g fractionated coconut oil
- 24 ounces pump bottle
- Fragrance variation
- 8 drops cypress essential oil.
- 10 drops sandalwood essential oil
- 10 drops white fir essential oil

Fragrance variation # 2:

- 45 ml rose water.
- 5 g beetroot powder (optional
- 30 g vegetable glycerin

Fragrance variation # 3:

- 12 drops lime essential oil
- 12 drops grapefruit essential oil
- 6 drops orange essential oil

Fragrance variation # 4

- 12 drops ylang-ylang essential oil
- 18 drops peppermint oil

Fragrance variation # 5:

- 30 drops any of your favorite essential oils (you can use a combination of oils)

Directions:
1. Pour castile soap into the pump bottle. Next, add the coconut oil followed by distilled water.
2. Choose any one of the above fragrance variations and add into the bottle.
3. Fasten the cap and shake the bottle until well combined.

52. Foaming Shave Soap

Ingredients and equipment:

- 100 ml liquid castile soap
- 100 ml warm distilled water
- 100 ml natural aloe Vera gel
- 30 g olive oil or almond oil
- 8 – 10 drops lavender oil or any other essential oil of your choice
- 5 g vitamin E oil
- 24 ounces pump bottle

Directions:

1. Pour castile soap into the pump bottle. Next, add the olive oil followed by aloe Vera and distilled water.
2. Add lavender oil and vitamin E oil into the bottle.
3. Fasten the cap and shake the bottle until well combined.

53. Vanilla Scented Liquid Soap

Ingredients:

- 2 bars castile soap (scentless)
- 6 liters clean distilled water
- 12 drops vanilla extract
- 60 ml coconut oil
- 1 large pot
- 1 cheese grater
- Dispensers

Directions:

1. Grate the bars of soap using the cheese grater.
2. Pour water in a large pot and keep on gas for boiling.
3. When water starts boiling, add the grated soap
4. Stir well until all the soap is completely melted.
5. Remove from heat and keep aside to cool for around 8 hours.
6. It would have thickened. Now add the vanilla extract and the coconut oil and stir well.
7. For a super smooth consistency, pass through a blender.
8. Pour into dispensers.

54. Orange And Mint Scented Soap

Ingredients:

- ½ bar castile soap (scentless)
- 1 ½ liters clean distilled water
- 3 drops orange essential oil
- 3 drops mint essential oil
- 15 g coconut oil
- 1 large pot
- 1 cheese grater
- Dispensers

Directions:

1. Grate the soap with the cheese grater.
2. Pour water in a large pot and place it for heating on the gas.
3. When the water starts boiling, add the soap.
4. Mix well until the soap is totally dissolved.
5. Set aside to cool and thicken for about 8 hours.
6. Now add the coconut oil, orange oil and mint oil. Stir well.
7. For a super smooth consistency pass through a blender.
8. Pour into dispensers.

55. Natural Homemade Baby Wash and Shampoo

Ingredients and equipment:

- 300 ml unscented liquid castile soap
- 60 ml almond oil or fractionated coconut oil
- 20 drops lavender essential oil
- 120 g vegetable glycerin
- 30 g aloe Vera juice (optional)
- 60 ml distilled water or filtered water
- 32 ounces pump bottle

Directions:

1. Pour liquid soap, almond oil, aloe Vera juice and glycerin, and lavender oil into the pump bottle.
2. Pour water on top. Fasten the lid and shake the bottle for 30 – 40 seconds or until well combined.
3. Use as a wash or shampoo for babies.

Conclusion

In the realm of crafting, there exists a captivating alchemy, an artistry that beckons individuals to explore the delicate dance between nature and creativity. Throughout the pages of "Natural Soap Making," we embarked on a journey into this world, discovering the nuanced symphony of elements that converge to create not just soap, but a sensorial experience that connects us to the earth and our own innate ingenuity.

At its core, this book sought to convey a fundamental truth: soap making is a sensory ode to nature, an homage to simplicity and purity. In traversing the chapters, we delved into the raw materials that constitute the heart of natural soap, understanding how botanicals, oils, and lye harmonize to birth a product that transcends mere cleanliness. This isn't just a utilitarian cleanse; it's a ritualistic embrace of nature's bounty.

The journey began with a primer on the history of soap making, unraveling the ancient tapestry woven by civilizations that recognized the profound union of science and art in crafting cleansing agents. From Babylonian concoctions to the Castilian soap of the 16th century, we witnessed the evolution of a practice that has stood the test of time, echoing through the ages with an enduring whisper of wisdom.

A cornerstone of this exploration was the revelation that natural soap making is not a rigid science but a fluid canvas awaiting the strokes of individuality. We navigated the vast landscape of oils, each with its unique properties, and botanicals that offered not just fragrance but therapeutic benefits. The chapters unfolded like petals, revealing the secrets of infusions, colorants, and essential oils, empowering the reader to paint their olfactory and visual masterpiece.

The chemistry of saponification was demystified, laying bare the transformative dance between oils and lye. Yet, in this dance, there was a plea for caution, an acknowledgment that mastery required respect for the materials at hand. Soap making, we learned, is both an art and a science—one that demands not just creativity but precision.

Amidst the discussions on molds, curing, and troubleshooting, a recurrent theme emerged—the celebration of imperfection. Natural soap making, we declared, is not about flawlessness but authenticity. Each bubble, swirl, and hue tells a story of the hands that crafted it. In the pursuit of perfection, one might lose the essence of the craft—a lesson applicable not just to soap making but to life's myriad pursuits.

As promised, this book extended beyond the technicalities of soap making; it embraced the ethos of a lifestyle. It wasn't just about concocting a cleansing agent; it was an invitation to slow down, breathe in the fragrant whispers of botanicals, and reconnect with a primal practice that transcends the hurried pace of modern existence. The solution presented was not a mere recipe; it was a prescription for mindfulness, an elixir to counterbalance the frenetic rhythms of contemporary life.

So, what is the one thing to carry forward from these pages, the distilled essence of "Natural Soap Making"? It is the understanding that within the seemingly simple act of crafting soap lies a profound alchemy—a fusion of science, art, and a dash of the divine. It is an acknowledgment that in a world inundated with synthetic commodities, there is an indescribable satisfaction in creating something pure and tangible with one's hands.

As the curtain falls on this exploration, let the reader depart not just with a head full of knowledge but with hands itching to create, eyes attuned to the beauty of imperfection, and a heart resonating with the rhythm of the earth. "Natural Soap Making" isn't merely a manual; it is a testament to the enduring allure of simplicity, the elegance of the handmade, and the perennial dance between nature and human ingenuity. So, go forth, dear reader, and let the suds of creativity cleanse not just your skin but your soul.

Printed in Great Britain
by Amazon